ROOTS AND WINGS: A HOLISTIC GUIDE TO RAISING VISIONARY, CURIOUS, AND COMPASSIONATE KIDS

DIPAK KHUSHALANI

To my wife Priyanka Khushalani, my love, my strength, and my greatest supporter—your unwavering belief in me has been the foundation of this journey. Your patience, encouragement, and love have made every late night and early morning worth it. I am endlessly grateful to walk this path with you.

To my precious daughters, Kiara Khushalani and Kyna Khushalani—you are the light of my life, the reason I dream bigger, and the inspiration behind every word in this book. Watching you grow fills my heart with boundless joy, and I hope this book becomes a small part of the beautiful world I wish to create for you.

I love you more than words can ever express. Always and forever.

Contents

Preface

Raising children is both the most rewarding and challenging journey a parent can embark on. In today's fast-paced, technology-driven world, it can often feel like the odds are stacked against us. We face the pressures of screen time, distractions, and the constant demand for our children's attention. But beneath these challenges lies the incredible opportunity to guide our children toward becoming curious, compassionate, and visionary individuals.

This book is born out of my deep love and commitment to raising my own daughters, Kiara and Kyna, in a world where they are not defined by screens, but by their creativity, emotional intelligence, and ability to think beyond the surface. As a father, educator, and lifelong learner, I've spent years reflecting on how we can cultivate these qualities in our children while navigating the demands of modern parenting.

In Roots and Wings, I share with you a holistic approach to raising children who are not only academically successful but also kind, curious, and equipped to tackle life's challenges. This book offers practical strategies for reducing screen time, fostering curiosity, and building emotional resilience, while emphasizing the importance of storytelling, mindfulness, and strong family connections.

My goal with this book is simple: to offer parents like you a roadmap for nurturing a generation of children who are prepared to lead with empathy, creativity, and a deep understanding of the world around them.

As you turn these pages, my hope is that you find inspiration, guidance, and the reassurance that, as parents, we are all capable of giving our children the best possible start in life. Together, we can help them spread their roots deep into the earth and grow wings that will take them far. Thank you for trusting me to be part of your parenting journey.

With all my love and gratitude,
Dipak Khushalani

Acknowledgements

Writing Roots and Wings has been a deeply personal journey, shaped by my experiences as a father, educator, and storyteller. This book would not have been possible without the unwavering support of my wife, who has been my pillar of strength, and my daughters, Kiara and Kyna, who inspire me every day with their curiosity and innocence.

A heartfelt thank you to my students, whose inquisitiveness has always reminded me of the importance of nurturing a child's natural hunger for learning. To my family and friends, especially my close friend Rushi, your encouragement and belief in me have been invaluable.

Finally, to every parent reading this book—thank you for choosing to embark on this journey of mindful parenting. The world needs more parents like you who are willing to nurture both the roots of strong values and the wings of boundless curiosity in their children.

Introduction

If you're reading this, chances are you have felt the struggle—the moment when your child chooses a screen over a conversation, a video over a book, or an endless scroll over real-world play. Maybe you're wondering how things got to this point. Maybe you have even asked yourself: Is it even possible to raise a child in today's world without them being glued to a screen?

The good news? Yes, it's possible. The even better news? That's just the beginning.

When I first set out to write this book, my focus was clear: help parents break their children's screen addiction. I wanted to provide practical, step-by-step strategies to help kids disengage from devices and rediscover real-life joys. But as I delved deeper, I realized something profound—screens are just one part of a much bigger issue.

The real challenge isn't just about limiting screen time. It's about shaping a child's mindset, emotions, and character. It's about nurturing curiosity, building resilience, fostering compassion, and instilling values like patience, honesty, and integrity. It's about helping children navigate negative emotions like jealousy, anger, procrastination, and frustration. It's about raising kids who are not only screen-free but also self-aware, emotionally intelligent, and deeply connected to their parents, their culture, and their values.

This book, therefore, is not just a guide to reducing screen time—it's a roadmap to holistic parenting.

Why Listen to Me?

I'm not a psychologist, nor do I have a PhD in parenting (does that even exist?). But I do have over 12 years of experience teaching thousands of students between the ages of 7 and 17. I have spent countless hours observing, guiding, and problem-solving for kids—watching them struggle, watching them grow, and helping them navigate their emotions, challenges, and aspirations. I have had deep conversations with parents, listening to their concerns about academics, behavior, peer pressure, and emotional struggles. I seen firsthand how mindsets are shaped, how confidence is built, and how negative emotions like jealousy, procrastination, and anger can be rewired into something positive with the right approach.

And then, I became a parent myself.

If I thought I understood childhood psychology before, parenting took my learning to an entirely new level. My daughters, Kiara (4) and Kyna (1), became my personal case studies in behavioral science. I wasn't just observing children from the outside—I was now inside the experiment, living every moment of growth, tantrums, learning, and unlearning.

How the Pandemic Changed Childhood.

The pandemic didn't just disrupt our lives; it reshaped childhood itself. Schools shut down, playgrounds became off-limits, and social interactions dwindled. In this vacuum, screens stepped in as both a savior and a silent disruptor.

Online schooling became the new normal, forcing kids to spend 4-5 hours a day in front of screens. Parents, working from home, unknowingly relied on digital entertainment to keep their children occupied. And so, an entire generation of kids was introduced to a world where screens were not just a source of entertainment but a necessity, a comfort zone, and—eventually—an addiction.

At first, it seemed harmless. But soon, the side effects began to surface.

Children became more irritable, less focused, and increasingly dependent on instant gratification. Attention spans shrank. Creativity declined. The natural joy of exploring, playing, and imagining was replaced by passive consumption.

But it wasn't just children who changed.

Parents, too, were affected. The excessive use of the internet and social media altered our own mindsets, emotions, and interactions. The fast-paced digital world made us more impatient, less present, and, in many cases, emotionally drained. And this, in turn, affected how we connected with our children.

I observed this pattern—not just in my own family, but in countless others. And that's when I realized: the problem is bigger than screen addiction.

Yes, we need to help our children reduce their screen time, but we also need to rebuild the lost connection between parents and kids. We need to equip our children with emotional intelligence, problem-solving skills, and a deep sense of self-awareness.

This book was born out of that realization.

A Practical, Actionable Guide for Parents.

I know that most parenting books are filled with theories, but this isn't one of them. This book is designed to be practical and effective from Day 1.

At the end of each chapter, you'll find clear, actionable strategies that you can apply immediately. These are not vague, philosophical ideas—they are concrete steps that will bring visible, measurable change in your child's behavior.

The book is structured into 19 chapters, each focusing on a critical aspect of childhood development. But here's my one request:

Do not read this book in one go.

Yes, you heard that right. Instead of rushing through, I urge you to read just one chapter at a time. Then, implement the actionable strategies given at the end of that chapter. Observe the results. See the changes in your child's behavior. Only after successfully applying the lessons from one chapter should you move on to the next.

Some chapters will be deeply introspective, making you reflect on your own childhood, parenting style, and personal growth. Some will challenge the way you think about raising kids. And some will give you simple, yet powerful tools that can transform your child's habits and mindset.

Parenting is a journey, not a checklist.

And this book is designed to guide you through that journey—one step at a time.

The Ultimate Goal: Raising a Generation of Empathetic, Visionary, and Strong-Minded Children.

The world today is filled with distractions, short attention spans, and a growing disconnect between people. If we, as parents, don't take charge now, the next generation could grow up lacking empathy, patience, and real-life problem-solving skills.

But here's the good news: You have the power to change that.

Parents are the architects of the future. The way we raise our children today will shape the society of tomorrow. If we instill the right values—compassion, integrity, curiosity, and resilience—we can create a generation that is not only successful but also emotionally strong, deeply connected, and truly fulfilled.

That is the purpose of this book.

Not just to help you remove screens from your child's life, but to help you raise a child who is visionary, curious, and compassionate—a child who has both roots and wings.

So, let's embark on this journey together.

Let's rediscover the lost art of parenting.

Let's give our children the tools they need to thrive—not just in a world of technology, but in a world of real human connections, deep values, and endless possibilities.

CHAPTER ONE

Transform

Breaking the Screen's Spell

Why Is Your Child So Glued to the Screen?

Picture this: Your child is sitting in front of a screen, utterly hypnotized. You could set off a firecracker, announce an all-you-can-eat chocolate buffet, or even summon a parade of puppies into the room, and they'd still remain unfazed—eyes locked, body still, mind completely absorbed in the glowing rectangle before them. Hunger? Ignored. Thirst? Secondary. The real world? Who cares?

Now, let's rewind a little.

Remember the shows we watched as kids? They weren't just a riot of colors and funny characters; they actually taught us something—kindness, teamwork, resilience. The creators of those shows were like wise elders wrapped in animated magic, subtly shaping our values through engaging storytelling. We laughed, we learned, and somehow, we still managed to play outside for hours.

Fast-forward to today, and we've swapped thoughtful storytelling for algorithm-fueled binge-watching. Unlike the scheduled TV slots we grew up with, today's digital platforms operate on one terrifyingly simple principle: keep them hooked. There's no "Come back next week for the next episode!" Instead, it's an infinite scroll of algorithm-fed content, ensuring that whatever your child watches next is exactly what will keep them watching longer. It's like handing them a plate of their favorite food and watching it magically refill every time they take a bite.

And the masterminds behind this? They aren't childhood development experts or educators. They're independent creators, influencers, and corporations chasing views, clicks, and ad revenue. The goal? Engagement at all costs. They don't care if your child learns a valuable lesson—they only care if they stay glued to the screen long enough to watch the next ad.

It's Not Just About "Bad Content"

The problem isn't just that kids today are watching junk (though, let's be honest, some of it makes even the most mind-numbing reality TV look like Shakespeare). The real problem is that screens are changing how kids experience the world.

I saw this firsthand in my own home.

One evening, I was watching my two daughters, Kiara and Kyna, while my wife was in the kitchen, whisking batter like she was on an intense episode of MasterChef. Kiara was sprawled on the sofa, locked into her favorite videos. Meanwhile, baby Kyna was busy entertaining herself—first with her toys, then with a pillow, and finally, in an ambitious act of discovery, with her own toes.

And then—it happened.

Kyna, in her curious little adventure, wriggled too close to the edge of the bed. One overenthusiastic kick, one wrong move, and... thud! The kind of cry that could shatter glass erupted from her tiny lungs.

I bolted to her side, my heart racing. But then, something even more alarming caught my attention.

Kiara, the doting elder sister who would normally rush to console her baby sibling, didn't even blink.

She didn't flinch. She didn't gasp. She didn't so much as look in Kyna's direction for more than a fleeting second before sinking back into her digital world.

It was like watching a scene from a dystopian sci-fi movie—a child so deeply sucked into the digital vortex that even real pain happening right in front of her barely registered. That moment shook me to my core.

This wasn't just screen time. This was screen dependence.

And I knew I had to do something.

The Science of the Screen Addiction: Why Kids Can't Look Away

Before you start blaming your child for being "lazy" or "obsessed with screens," let's get one thing straight—it's not their fault.

The real villains here? The tech wizards who've engineered this addiction.

Modern content creators are basically digital drug dealers, crafting the perfect recipe to keep kids coming back for more. They use every psychological trick in the book to make sure once your child starts watching, stopping feels nearly impossible.

Here's how they do it:

1. Rapid Scene Changes

The brain loves novelty. Digital content bombards kids with fast cuts and constant motion, keeping their attention locked in like a moth to a flame.

2. High-Saturation Colors

Neon blues! Fiery reds! Hypnotic pinks! These colors trigger dopamine—the brain's pleasure chemical—making screens more stimulating than reality.

3. Catchy Jingles & Repetitive Music

Ever wondered why some kids' songs are so irritatingly catchy? It's intentional. Repetition reinforces memory, making kids crave the familiar beats over and over again.

4. Cliffhangers & Suspense

Ending an episode mid-action ensures your child has to keep watching. It's like reading a book that refuses to let you put it down.

5. Personalized Algorithm Traps

Once a child watches one funny cat video, the algorithm bombards them with a thousand more, locking them into a never-ending loop of similar content.

6. No Downtime

Unlike books or playtime, where natural pauses allow the brain to breathe, digital content flows continuously, overwhelming kids with constant stimulation.

7. Interactive Elements

Videos that ask, "What should happen next?" make kids feel engaged—like they're in control—when in reality, they're being expertly manipulated.

8. Simple, Predictable Storylines

Nothing too complicated, nothing too deep—just easy, digestible, dopamine-driven stories designed to keep them watching longer.

All of these elements create an environment that's more stimulating than real life. And here's the dangerous part: once kids get used to this level of constant excitement, the real world starts to feel boring in comparison.

This isn't just fascination. It's neurological conditioning.

How to Break the Spell (Without World War III at Home) So, what do you do?

Here's what doesn't work:

? Yelling: "TURN THAT THING OFF RIGHT NOW!" (Unless you want to start a tantrum worthy of a Shakespearean tragedy.)

? Snatching the device away like a referee confiscating an illegal move. (Enjoy the emotional explosion that follows.)

? Offering the real world as a bland alternative. ("Stop watching that! Here, stare at this beige wall instead.")

Instead, try this:

1. Start with Becoming Their Co-Viewer

Plop yourself on the couch and pretend you're the biggest fan of their show. Ask questions like, "Wait, why does this talking dog have superpowers?" or "Who's the villain here? Are they misunderstood?" Why? Because once you engage, they start seeing you as part of their world again.

2. Turn Screen Themes into Real-Life Adventures

If they're obsessed with a show about jungle adventures—turn the backyard into a safari. If they're watching baking videos—whip out the flour and bake something for real.

3. Make Reality Just as Exciting

Kids aren't addicted to screens. They're addicted to engagement. If we make the real world just as engaging (without resorting to juggling fire), they'll want to participate.

4. Replace, Don't Just Remove

Don't just take screens away. Offer something better. If they're watching superheroes, hand them a cape and say, "Let's save the world outside."

The Real Takeaway

Your child isn't broken. They're just responding to a system designed to keep them watching.

Our job as parents isn't to ban screens—it's to make the real world so compelling that screens become just one of many exciting options.

This book isn't here to preach at you. It's here to give you real, practical ways to help your child find balance—without screaming matches, guilt trips, or dramatic power struggles.

And trust me, by the time you finish this book, you'll be so glad you picked it up.

• 5 •

CHAPTER TWO

Mind Control

The Illusion of Free Will

Let's admit it.

Most of us walk around feeling like we're the main characters of life, making independent, informed decisions as we march confidently toward our destiny. We believe our thoughts are our own, our choices are deliberate, and our desires are authentic. We like to think we're free thinkers, unshackled by influence, consciously navigating life based on what we want.

But what if I told you that most of what you believe to be your own thoughts aren't really yours?

What if I told you that your decisions—what to eat, what to wear, what to watch, what to believe, who to admire, even what to fear—are not the product of your own independent reasoning, but the result of a meticulously crafted system that has been shaping your mind since childhood?

Sounds dramatic, right?

Like some sci-fi dystopian thriller where a shadowy organization is pulling the strings behind the scenes. But the truth is, the puppeteers don't wear black coats and meet in secret underground lairs. They don't have to. They exist in plain sight—on your screen, in your pocket, in the advertisements you barely notice, in the news you scroll past, in the childhood stories that were read to you, and in the seemingly harmless suggestions whispered into your ears by algorithms that know you better than you know yourself.

Think about it.

Have you ever caught yourself impulsively buying a product you never planned to own, just because it kept showing up on your feed? Have you ever found yourself binge-watching an entire season of a show you had zero intention of starting, just because Netflix played the next episode before you could escape? Or worse—have you ever adopted a belief, a preference, or even a fear, only to realize later that you don't know why you believe it in the first place?

This isn't just random coincidence. It's not just "modern life." It's the result of a system that thrives on influencing you without you realizing it.

And if you think this only applies to adults, think again. Because if we, as grown-ups with years of life experience,can be so easily manipulated, imagine what's happening to our children.

The Puppet Masters

Welcome to the age of the algorithm, where your thoughts, impulses, and desires are being carefully guided without you ever noticing.

Every click, every scroll, every like and share—it's all data. That pizza place you Googled last week? Logged. The meme you laughed at for a little too long? Noted. That one time you searched "how to be more productive" at 2 a.m.? The system saw that too.

And guess what? This data isn't just sitting in a digital vault somewhere, collecting virtual dust. It's being fed into hyper-intelligent systems designed not to serve you, but to predict you, influence you, and, in many cases, control you.

That's why, the next time you open your phone, you'll see an ad for that thing you swear you only thought about but never actually searched. That's why your social media feed isn't filled with random content, but an eerily specific, hand-tailored stream of posts designed to keep you scrolling. That's why, after just one YouTube video about minimalism, your recommendations suddenly assume you're about to sell all your possessions and move into a tiny home in the woods.

The algorithm isn't just watching you—it's sculpting you.

It's not just about products; it's about beliefs.

It's about nudging you toward certain viewpoints, reinforcing ideas you've barely questioned, and surrounding you with content that feels like your own thoughts, when in reality, it's just an echo of the system's agenda.

And here's the scary part: it's been happening since before you even knew what an algorithm was.

The Silent Programming

Long before the internet, before smartphones, before social media, we were already being programmed. It started in childhood, with the stories we were told, the media we consumed, and the narratives that were repeated so often that they became truth in our minds.

Think about it.

Who decided that pink is for girls and blue is for boys?

Who taught you that success means getting good grades, landing a secure job, and following a predetermined path?

Who told you that some dreams are "realistic" and others are "too risky"?

Why do you crave social validation? Why do you feel anxious when your phone is out of reach? Why do you instinctively trust some sources of information while dismissing others?

These thoughts didn't just appear in your mind. They were planted there.

The education system, the media, the culture we grew up in—all of them played a role in shaping how we think. They established the foundation. And now, in the digital age, the algorithm has taken over where tradition left off.

But here's the real danger: at least in the past, the shaping of our minds happened over years, decades, even generations. Now, it happens in real time, at an unimaginable speed, with artificial intelligence analyzing and adjusting its influence on you every second you're online.

And if we, as adults, are struggling to reclaim our thoughts, how can we expect children—whose minds are still forming—to stand a chance?

The Battle for Awareness

Most people go through life never realizing that their thoughts aren't entirely their own.

But once you do realize it, something shifts. It's like stepping out of The Matrix, like seeing the code behind reality. Suddenly, you start questioning things that never even seemed questionable before.

You begin to wonder:

"Do I really want this, or was I made to want it?"

"Do I really believe this, or was I taught to believe it?"

"Is this my thought, or is it something I absorbed without realizing it?"

And this is the turning point.

Because once you start asking these questions, you begin to reclaim ownership over your mind. You start making choices consciously, rather than just following the invisible strings that have been pulling you along.

And if we, as parents, can wake up to this reality, we can start protecting our children from falling even deeper into the illusion.

This isn't about demonizing technology. It's about awareness.

It's about recognizing that the world our children are growing up in is designed to shape their minds before they even know they have a choice. It's about understanding that they don't stand a chance unless we guide them toward critical thinking, conscious decision-making, and an awareness of the invisible forces trying to mold them.

Because if we don't, the screen will.

The algorithm isn't raising conscious, independent thinkers. It's raising passive consumers, locked in a cycle of endless scrolling, mindless watching, and automatic acceptance.

But here's the good news: once you know what you don't know, you can start changing it.

So, the question is—are you ready to take back control?

Because what comes next is the blueprint for doing just that.

And trust me—you're about to see the world very differently.

The Real Casualties: Our Kids

Now, let's talk about the ones who stand to lose the most—our kids. If we, with all our "maturity" and "critical thinking," are falling prey to this digital puppet show, what chance do they have?

The Emotional Depth of a Story vs. The Chaos of Short Videos

When we watch a powerful movie, something incredible happens—we don't just see a story unfold; we become part of it. A well-crafted film takes us on an emotional journey, allowing us to feel the pain, struggles, and triumphs of the protagonist. As the story progresses, we witness their transformation—how they grow, how they overcome obstacles, and how their journey reshapes our own perspective on life. These emotions stay with us long after the credits roll, subtly influencing our thoughts and shaping our understanding of the world.

Now, compare this to the rapid, mindless consumption of short-form content on YouTube Shorts, Instagram Reels, and TikTok. Here, every 30 seconds (or less), a new video appears—completely different from the last. One moment, we are watching a heartfelt reunion; the next, a prank; then, a dance clip, followed by a piece of tragic news, and suddenly a comedy skit. The brain, caught in this whirlwind, barely processes one emotion before being slammed with another. This constant emotional turbulence creates imbalance, confusion, and detachment. Unlike a movie, where emotions are built gradually and meaningfully, short videos force our brains to jump from joy to shock to laughter to sadness within seconds—something human cognition was never designed to handle.

This overstimulation leads to emotional numbness. People become desensitized, unable to deeply engage with real emotions. They laugh without truly feeling joy, feel sadness without processing why, and experience anger without understanding its root. Instead of deep thinkers, we create zombies—passive consumers who are constantly entertained but never truly moved, constantly watching but never truly understanding.

The contrast is striking:

A movie nourishes the mind, while short videos flood it with noise. One builds empathy and insight; the other shatters emotional stability. The choice is ours—whether to immerse ourselves in meaningful stories or let fragmented content erode our ability to feel, think, and connect.

We grew up in a world where childhood meant scraped knees, tree-climbing adventures, and awkward first crushes. But today's kids? They're growing up in a world where their experiences are curated by algorithms, their opinions are shaped by influencers, and their desires are engineered by data-driven marketing.

Their lessons aren't coming from real-life mistakes and face-to-face conversations. They're learning from YouTube ads, TikTok trends, and unboxing videos. Their idea of happiness? A new gadget. Their idea of success? Likes and followers. Their idea of connection? Heart emojis on a screen.

It's not just screen addiction—it's an entirely new way of thinking. One that makes instant gratification more appealing than patience, consumption more important than creation, and validation from strangers more meaningful than self-worth.

And if that doesn't keep us up at night, what will?

The Digital Prison

Let's call it what it is: a digital prison. And unlike a traditional one, this one doesn't have bars or guards—it has autoplay, notifications, and endless scrolling. It's not just locking kids in; it's locking out everything that makes childhood magical: imagination, curiosity, and real-world connection.

This is the new normal:

• A child is more likely to recognize a YouTube influencer than a historical figure.

• A toddler learns to swipe before they learn to hold a pencil.

• A teenager panics if their phone battery hits 10% but never checks in on their own mental well-being.

And the worst part? We're handing them the keys to this prison every time we give them a screen to keep them occupied.

But this isn't about guilt. It's about awareness. We can still change this.

Breaking Free: A Parent's Playbook

So, how do we protect our kids? How do we raise them to think for themselves in a world that's trying to do the thinking for them?

The answer isn't to ban technology—it's to teach them how to use it consciously, critically, and with control.

Here's how we start:

1. Teach Them to Question Everything

Algorithms thrive on passive consumers. The first step to breaking free is teaching our kids to question what they see.

Encourage them to ask:

? Who benefits if I watch this?

? Why is this being suggested to me?

? Is this real, or is it designed to get my attention?

Turn this into a game. When they see an ad, ask them, "What's the trick here?" When they watch a viral trend, challenge them to find out why it became popular. Make them detectives of the digital world.

The goal isn't to make them skeptical—it's to make them aware.

2. Create Screen-Free Rituals

A child who knows the joy of real-world experiences will naturally crave more than just screen time.

? Dinner without distractions—Phones down, real conversations up.

? Weekly 'Analog Days'—A full day with no screens. Board games, hikes, storytelling, cooking together.

? Tech-free mornings and nights—Start and end the day without the dopamine rush of a screen.

The more they experience real life, the less they'll seek validation from the digital one.

3. Be the Role Model

We can't expect kids to limit their screen time while we're glued to ours. If we want them to engage in real conversations, we have to lead by example.

Try this:

• Replace scrolling with reading in front of them.

• Keep your phone away during meals and family time.

• Instead of immediately Googling something, discuss it first and try to find the answer together.

Children don't listen to what we say as much as they watch what we do.

4. Help Them Become Creators, Not Just Consumers

Instead of just watching videos, encourage them to make something. Instead of mindlessly scrolling, get them to write, draw, build, or explore.

Ideas to spark creativity:

? Start a journal or sketchbook.

? Encourage them to create stories instead of just watching them.

? Challenge them to make something from scratch—be it art, music, or even a simple comic strip.

When kids realize they can create, their dependency on consuming weakens.

5. Equip Them with Digital Literacy

Knowledge is power. The more our kids understand how the digital world operates, the less likely they are to fall for its traps.

Teach them:

? How algorithms work—Explain why their social media feed isn't random.

? The business behind content—Help them see how influencers and ads profit from attention.

? Privacy matters—Show them what data is collected and why protecting it is important.

A child who understands technology isn't afraid of it—but they also don't blindly follow it.

6. Demand Accountability from Big Tech

This isn't just a personal battle—it's a societal one.

Big tech companies profit from keeping kids glued to screens. They need to be held responsible.

As parents, we can:

? Advocate for ethical technology policies.

? Support laws that protect kids from addictive design.

? Push for transparency in how data is collected and used.

We don't have to accept the system as it is—we can demand change.

The Bigger Picture

This isn't just about our kids.

This is about the future of humanity.

If we allow technology to manipulate unchecked, we risk raising a generation that:

? Struggles to think for themselves.

? Values convenience over depth.

? Seeks validation instead of meaning.

But if we take action now, we can raise a generation that:

? Thinks critically, not passively.

? Values real-world connections over digital ones.

? Uses technology as a tool, not as a crutch.

This isn't about rejecting technology—it's about reclaiming control.

The choice is ours:

Do we allow screens to raise our kids?

Or do we step up, unplug, and show them what real life is?

If this chapter resonated with you, share it. Let's start a conversation. Let's wake up more parents. Let's make sure our kids own their minds—before the world programs them otherwise.

The future is watching. What will we do?

CHAPTER THREE

The Great Illusion

Wake up. Seriously, wake up!

Look around. Heads down. Eyes glued to screens. Fingers scrolling endlessly. Why? Because social media has hijacked our brains, feeding us a steady drip of dopamine—like a slot machine designed to keep us hooked. Every like, every share, every new post keeps us coming back for more.

But let's get real for a second. What are we actually consuming?

We see polished travel photos, aesthetic meals, perfect families, and grand celebrations. It looks real, right? After all, these aren't movie stars playing roles; they're our friends, colleagues, and influencers who seem to have it all together.

That's why it feels real. And that's why it hurts when we compare our ordinary, messy lives to these picture-perfect moments.

But here's the truth: It's all scripted.

The Script We Don't See

Think about it:

• The breathtaking beach photo? It took 50 tries to get the right angle.

• The "candid" laughter at brunch? Staged for the camera.

• The inspirational post about "loving life"? Maybe written on a bad day to maintain their 'personal brand.'

Everything you see is edited, filtered, and carefully chosen. The messy moments—the ones that make us human—get deleted.

And yet, we fall for it. We compare our reality to someone else's highlight reel. We measure our success, happiness, and self-worth against a fictional version of life that doesn't exist.

No wonder so many of us feel like we're falling behind.

Now, if we—grown adults with so-called maturity and critical thinking—are getting manipulated, imagine what's happening to our kids.

The Real Victims: Our Kids

Children today are growing up in a world where social media doesn't just entertain—it shapes their entire identity.

- They believe happiness comes from vacations and shopping hauls.
- They think beauty equals filters and angles.
- They chase likes as if they define self-worth.

Worst of all? They don't know any better. To them, this digital illusion is reality.

And that's terrifying. Because instead of exploring the world with curiosity, confidence, and authenticity, they're being conditioned to:

- Compare themselves constantly.
- Seek validation online.
- Struggle with self-worth when they can't keep up with the impossible standards they see.

If we don't wake up now, we're raising a generation that won't know who they truly are without a screen telling them.

Breaking Free: A Reality Check

So, what can we do? How do we protect our kids—and ourselves—from falling into this digital trap?

Here's how we take back control:

1. Understand the Illusion

Teach yourself (and your kids) to question everything they see online.

- Who benefits from this post?
- Why does this look so perfect?
- What's being hidden behind the camera?

When we remind ourselves that social media is a performance, not reality, we stop feeling inadequate. We stop comparing. And we stop letting a fake world dictate how we feel.

2. Build a Stronger Offline Connection

If our kids don't find a sense of belonging in the real world, they'll seek it online. That's where the real danger begins.

- Be present—not just physically, but emotionally.
- Create moments that don't need to be posted—family dinners, bedtime talks, spontaneous adventures.

• Talk openly about their feelings, insecurities, and struggles before they turn to social media for validation.

Your child should never feel like a screen understands them better than you do.

3. Set Digital Boundaries

• No screens at the dinner table. Conversations over notifications.

• No mindless scrolling before bed. Replace it with reading, storytelling, or simply unwinding together.

• No comparing real life to online life. Teach them to admire moments, not just Instagram posts.

Small changes can protect their mental well-being in a big way.

4. Teach Them to Question Trends

Kids are highly impressionable. Today's viral trend becomes tomorrow's obsession.

• Explain how influencers profit from engagement.

• Show them how companies manipulate emotions to sell products.

• Help them recognize when they're being influenced rather than making choices for themselves.

When they understand that social media isn't a mirror—it's a marketplace, they'll learn to engage with it more wisely.

5. Be the Example

If we're constantly checking our phones, what message are we sending?

• If we glorify social media, they will too.

• If we chase likes, they'll do the same.

• If we're present in real life, they'll learn to be as well.

Our kids don't need another lecture. They need to see us living the values we preach.

This isn't just about quitting social media. It's about reclaiming reality. It's about refusing to let a fictional, manipulated world define our happiness.

It's about teaching our kids to live fully, not just perform online.

Because at the end of the day, when all the screens are off, the only thing that truly matters is the life we've actually lived.

So, what's it going to be?

Are we going to keep letting algorithms dictate our self-worth?

Or are we going to unplug, wake up, and start living on our own terms?

The choice is yours.

CHAPTER FOUR

The Mirror Effect

From the moment they take their first breath, children are watching. Observing. Absorbing. Every movement, every reaction, every habit—we are their first teachers, whether we realize it or not.

If life were a movie, their eyes and ears would be the high-definition cameras and boom mics, capturing everything to piece together their understanding of the world. And here's the critical truth: they don't learn from what we tell them. They learn from what we show them.

The Science Behind Imitation

Psychologist Albert Bandura, a pioneer in behavioral psychology, demonstrated just how powerful this imitation mechanism is. His famous Bobo doll experiment revealed that children mimic behaviors they observe, especially when those behaviors appear rewarding.

He introduced Social Learning Theory, which explains that children acquire new habits not just through direct teaching but primarily through observation, imitation, and modeling. In simpler terms:

• They see. They copy. They repeat.

If they see kindness, they learn kindness. If they see anger, they learn anger. And if they see their parents glued to screens, guess what happens?

The Modern-Day Role Models: Screens

Let's be honest—screens have quietly replaced traditional role models in our children's lives. Bright colors, catchy sounds, endless animations—it's a digital carnival, and every tap is a free ride.

Bandura's concept of reciprocal determinism explains how this cycle deepens:

• The child wants the screen.
• The environment enables it.

• The behavior gets reinforced.

It's a loop, a trap, a hamster wheel where the child keeps running, but real-life experiences get left behind. The world outside becomes dull compared to the excitement of the screen.

But here's the part we don't talk about enough:

This cycle doesn't just affect kids. It affects us too.

Think about it—how often do we reach for our phones during meals, scroll mindlessly during conversations, or lose track of time watching short videos? Our children are watching. We are unknowingly teaching them that screens deserve attention more than people.

Breaking the Cycle (Without a War at Home)

Now, before you panic, let's be realistic. Breaking this habit isn't an overnight switch—it's more like changing an old, worn-out pair of shoes. It feels uncomfortable at first. It takes time to adjust. And yes, there will be resistance.

Your child won't throw the tablet away and start painting the next Mona Lisa overnight. But every tiny shift—five extra minutes outside, one less video before bed, one more meaningful conversation—adds up.

The goal isn't to eliminate screens entirely. It's to reshape the relationship your child has with them. Instead of screens being the default, they become a tool. Instead of passive consumption, we create active engagement with the real world.

What's Next? The Game Plan

You're not in this alone. In the next section, I'll share practical, hands-on strategies to build a screen-free environment your child will love—a world so engaging, so full of curiosity and joy, that they won't even miss the screen.

And here's the secret: it starts with us.

Let's show them a world worth looking up for.

Action Plan:

The Gift of an Unplugged Day Outdoors

Here's your corporate-style blueprint for a screen-free, nature-filled day that feels less like a parenting task and more like an executive retreat for your family.

The goal?

Strengthen emotional bonds, reduce screen reliance, and transform parenting into a fulfilling journey rather than another KPI to meet.

Project Name: Operation Unplugged Bliss

Objective:

To create a seamless, distraction-free outdoor experience that fosters emotional well-being and deeper parent-child connections—without feeling forced or overwhelming.

1. Project Kick-Off: Thoughtful Planning

Mission: Choose a stress-free location that invites relaxation and curiosity.

✓ Destination Options:

• A quiet park, serene lake, or a botanical garden within 30–60 minutes of home.

• A forest area for a mini-adventure or a petting zoo for hands-on interaction.

? Avoid: Crowded tourist hotspots or long GPS-dependent road trips—this isn't about logistics, it's about presence.

? Key Deliverable: A location that feels like an escape but doesn't require a detailed itinerary.

2. Resource Management: Pack Simple, Comforting Food

Mission: Keep meals homemade, easy, and free from distractions.

✓ Menu Suggestions:

• Breakfast: Fresh fruit, veggie sandwiches, or homemade smoothies.

• Lunch: Chapati rolls, stuffed parathas, or a simple one-pot rice dish.

• Extras: Cookies, nuts, and a thermos of chai or coffee (because you deserve it).

Pro Tip: Food is more than sustenance—it's a conversation starter. Sit together, eat slowly, and let your child lead the discussion.

? Key Deliverable: A meal plan that minimizes interruptions and maximizes connection.

3. Stakeholder Alignment: Be Fully Present

Mission: Treat this outing like a high-priority offsite—no multitasking allowed.

✓ Preparation: Inform colleagues or teams (if needed) that you're unplugging for the day.

✓ Guidelines:

• Phones are for emergencies or capturing memories—not emails, social media, or news updates.

• Both parents participate equally—this isn't a "one-parent-handles-it" kind of day.

? Key Deliverable: Your child feels like the center of your world, not an afterthought in your schedule.

4. Time Management: Embrace Simplicity

Mission: Let the day flow naturally rather than following a strict plan.

✓ Keep the agenda light: One location, flexible activities.

✓ Encourage free play:

• Skipping stones
• Bird-watching
• Cloud-gazing
• Storytelling

Pro Tip: Let your child set the pace. If they want to spend 20 minutes watching ants, let them. This is their moment of discovery.

? Key Deliverable: A relaxed, free-flowing day where time slows down and connections deepen.

5. Value Addition: Create Lasting Memories

Mission: Make this outing enriching, fun, and unforgettable.

✓ Activities to Engage the Senses:

• Play classic childhood games (hide-and-seek, tag, or simple obstacle races).

• Teach your child fun nature facts (which tree has the biggest leaves? Why do birds chirp more in the morning?).

• Share your childhood stories—the ones that made you laugh, wonder, or feel brave.

? Key Deliverable: Moments of shared joy and learning that outshine any screen.

6. Stress Mitigation: Leave Worries Behind

Mission: Make the day as relaxing for you as it is for your child.

✓ Leave deadlines, emails, and to-do lists at home.

✓ Practice mindfulness: Pay attention to the sound of rustling leaves, your child's laughter, and the warmth of the sun.

Pro Tip: This is not just for your child's well-being—it's your mental reset, too.

? Key Deliverable: A day that refreshes both you and your child—not just another item on your parenting to-do list.

Why This Works

✓ Emotional Impact: Uninterrupted time builds trust, security, and love.

✓ Digital Detox: Nature resets the overstimulated mind, replacing pixels with real-world magic.

✓ Lasting Memories: These small, intentional moments will be childhood highlights they carry forever.

Pro Tip for Long-Term Success

• Repeat this monthly—treat it like your family's "team-building retreat."

• Keep a journal of these outings—record your child's favorite moments, new learnings, and unexpected joys.

Final Deliverable: A happier, screen-free family bond that grows stronger over time.

Beyond One Day: The Long-Term Strategy

Your goal isn't just to detox your child for a day—it's to rewire their world so screens no longer feel like the only source of fun.

Phase 1: Post-Outing Detoxification

✓ Nature Connection: Start a miniature garden with your child—let them pick the plants and water them daily.

✓ Hands-on Responsibility: Introduce a small fish tank—caring for fish teaches patience and empathy.

✓ Creativity Boost: Collect leaves, pebbles, or sand from your outing and turn them into art or a memory scrapbook.

Phase 2: Regular Integration into Daily Life

✓ Start small: 2–3 screen-free activities per week.

✓ Let your child choose: Gardening, painting, building, storytelling—find what excites them.

✓ Keep it flexible: No forced schedules—follow their curiosity.

Phase 3: Building a Safe Emotional Space

✓ No scolding: Let mistakes be part of learning—avoid frustration if they lose interest or struggle.

✓ Celebrate small wins: Their first planted sapling? A funny drawing? Acknowledge it all.

✓ Be involved: Don't just supervise—participate. Be a companion, not just a guide.

Phase 4: Emotional Anchoring for Long-Term Impact

✓ Storytelling: Tie activities to fun anecdotes or traditions from your own childhood.

✓ Use humor: Laugh with them—make even failed attempts joyful.

✓ End on a high note: Whether it's a group hug, a small reward, or a special snack—wrap up every activity with warmth.

Phase 5: Scaling Up to a Screen-Free Lifestyle

✓ Monthly Family Challenge: Pick one big outdoor activity per month—hiking, kite flying, or visiting a farm.

✓ Seasonal Themes: Adapt with nature—rainy-day puddle play, winter bonfires, summer night stargazing.

✓ Milestone Rewards: Celebrate achievements—turn them into family traditions.

Final Thought: Building a Legacy, Not Just a Habit

This isn't just about breaking screen addiction. It's about building a childhood filled with wonder, curiosity, and deep family bonds.

Every outing, every shared laugh, every unplugged moment—this is what your child will remember. Not the latest app. Not the trending video. But the real-world magic you created for them.

Start small. Stay consistent. And watch your child's world bloom—one unplugged day at a time.

CHAPTER FIVE

Fostering Curiosity: From Wonder to Discovery

The real world has endless wonders to offer—far more than a six-inch screen ever could. But for a child captivated by screens and the fantasy of reels, this isn't a realization that comes overnight.

As parents, we need to believe in our efforts and understand that this is a journey, not a quick fix. Each small step we take to engage a child away from the screen is progress. The goal is to help them discover something more exciting in the real world—something they choose to pursue, leaving the screen behind naturally.

So, how do we achieve this?

It's easy to feel limited. You can't go on picnics every day. You can't set aside all your responsibilities to entertain your child endlessly. Even the toys you've carefully chosen might not hold their interest for long. This frustration often leads to handing them a screen, followed by guilt for not nurturing their full potential.

But here's the truth: you don't have to be with your child every second or constantly provide extravagant activities. With a slight shift in perspective, you'll find countless opportunities right around you.

Let me share with you an inspiring story from history—the childhood of Dr. Vikram Sarabhai, a name synonymous with India's space program. Dr. Sarabhai, often celebrated as the father of Indian space exploration, was not just a scientist but a visionary whose efforts paved the way for India to emerge as a global leader in science and technology. Born on August 12, 1919, in Ahmedabad, Gujarat, Vikram Sarabhai grew up in an extraordinary environment that nurtured his innate curiosity and thirst for knowledge.

The Sarabhai family was one of Ahmedabad's most distinguished households, renowned for their philanthropy and commitment to education and societal progress. Their home was not just a residence but a vibrant hub of intellectual conversations, frequented by thinkers, artists, and scientists. Imagine a young Vikram, surrounded by this rich tapestry of ideas and discussions, absorbing every word, and letting his imagination soar.

From a very early age, Vikram's curiosity was evident to everyone around him. He wasn't the kind of child who accepted things at face value. If he encountered a phenomenon, a device, or even an idea, he wouldn't rest until he had explored the "why" and "how" behind it. His questions were never superficial—they were probing, insightful, and often left adults around him in awe of his ability to think deeply.

One particular story from his childhood illustrates this perfectly. At the age of ten, Vikram developed a fascination for clocks. He wasn't satisfied with merely watching the hands tick or listening to their rhythmic chime. No, young Vikram wanted to know what made a clock tick—literally. So, one day, he took apart an old family clock, piece by piece, trying to uncover the secrets of its intricate machinery. Of course, as you might expect, reassembling it was a different challenge altogether. But here's the remarkable part—his parents didn't scold him. Instead, they encouraged his curiosity and helped him understand how the clock worked. This moment was a turning point, teaching Vikram that exploration and even mistakes are essential steps in the journey of learning.

His curiosity wasn't limited to mechanical objects. Vikram was equally captivated by nature. He would spend hours in his family's lush garden, observing the patterns in leaves, the behavior of insects, and the subtle changes in plants with the seasons. What stood out was his instinct to experiment—testing how plants reacted to varying amounts of water or sunlight. These early, seemingly simple experiments laid the foundation for the scientific rigor and love for discovery that would define his life's work.

His parents, recognizing the spark in their son, ensured he had access to books, scientific tools, and mentors who could guide his insatiable curiosity. They also instilled in him the values of self-discovery and exploration, inspired by the teachings of Rabindranath Tagore and Mahatma Gandhi. These values became the cornerstones of his personality, shaping him into a thinker who always sought solutions that could benefit society.

Even in school, Vikram stood out. While other children were content to memorize facts, Vikram challenged the status quo. He wanted to understand the principles behind what he was taught. His questions often pushed his teachers to think deeper and explore new ways of explaining concepts.

This relentless drive to question and learn became a defining feature of his academic and professional journey.

These formative years of curiosity, encouragement, and exploration were instrumental in shaping Vikram Sarabhai into the visionary leader he would become. His ability to think beyond the obvious and approach problems with creativity and determination led to the establishment of ISRO and numerous other institutions that continue to impact India's scientific and technological progress.

As parents and educators, there's a powerful lesson in Vikram Sarabhai's childhood. Nurturing curiosity, encouraging questions, and providing an environment where exploration is celebrated can unlock the incredible potential in every child. The story of Vikram Sarabhai reminds us that it is curiosity that lights the spark of innovation, and innovation that transforms the future.

Let me share with you one more inspiring story.

story of James Clerk Maxwell, a name etched in history as one of the most brilliant minds in the world of science. Born in 1831 in Edinburgh, Scotland, Maxwell grew up in a family that deeply valued education and intellectual curiosity. From an early age, Maxwell's fascination with the mysteries of nature set him apart. His childhood wasn't just a phase of playful exploration—it was a foundation for discoveries that would change the world forever.

Even as a young boy, Maxwell's curiosity was insatiable. While most children his age were busy with simple games, Maxwell's mind was occupied with questions about how the world worked. By the age of eight, he was already probing into the complexities of the physical world, showcasing an extraordinary ability to grasp ideas far beyond his years. Teachers often marveled at his passion for geometry and mathematics, but it was his drive to understand the "why" behind phenomena that truly set him apart.

One of the defining moments of Maxwell's early life was his fascination with light and color. While others were content to observe the beauty of nature, Maxwell sought to uncover the science behind it. At just 14 years old, he began experimenting with colored papers, curious about how they interacted with light. What started as a simple observation turned into something profound. Maxwell began theorizing that color could be understood as a combination of three primary colors: red, green, and blue. This revolutionary idea, born from a teenager's curiosity, would later become the foundation for modern color science and technology, including the screens we use today. His first scientific paper, written on this very subject, marked the beginning of a lifelong journey of discovery.

Maxwell's exploration of light and color wasn't just a passing interest; it became the stepping stone for his groundbreaking work in electromagnetism. By the age of 16, he had entered the University of Edinburgh, where his curiosity only deepened. His early experiments had taught him to see connections where others saw none, and this ability led him to question the relationship between electricity and magnetism. In his twenties, Maxwell formulated the now-famous equations that describe how electric and magnetic fields interact—a discovery that reshaped the very foundation of physics.

These equations, which revealed that light itself is an electromagnetic wave, didn't just answer long-standing scientific questions. They paved the way for revolutionary technologies like radio, television, and wireless communication, transforming how we live and connect with the world. It's awe-inspiring to think that such monumental discoveries began with the simple, curious questions of a young boy experimenting with light and color.

Maxwell's journey from a curious child to a pioneering scientist is a powerful reminder of what curiosity can achieve. His ability to question the ordinary and seek deeper truths led to discoveries that have shaped our modern world. His childhood experiments, far from being trivial, were the seeds of world-changing insights. They remind us that even the simplest questions, when pursued with determination, can illuminate the path to groundbreaking discoveries.

As we reflect on Maxwell's life, we see the boundless potential of nurturing curiosity. His story is a testament to the power of wonder, the importance of exploration, and the transformative impact of a curious mind. It's a reminder that within every child lies the potential to unlock the secrets of the universe, and that fostering this curiosity can lead to innovations that shape the future in unimaginable ways.

As a Physics teacher, I've always been deeply fascinated by the childhood stories of great scientists. It's not just about their discoveries or the theories they've gifted the world—it's about understanding the spark that set their journey in motion.

What were they like as children?

What fueled their curiosity?

What inspired them to question, to experiment, and ultimately, to revolutionize the way we see the universe?

For me, uncovering these stories isn't just a passion—it's a way to connect with the next generation. I believe that every child holds immense potential, and the tales of these scientific legends can ignite that same curiosity and drive. By sharing the childhood experiences of scientists like James Clerk Maxwell or Dr. Vikram Sarabhai, I hope to inspire my students and readers to see themselves in these stories, to realize that greatness often begins with a simple question or a spark of curiosity.

It's this passion for understanding the beginnings of brilliance that drives me to delve deeper into their lives. As a teacher, I feel a responsibility to pass on these stories, to show that the path to innovation isn't reserved for a chosen few. It's a journey of wonder, exploration, and persistence—a journey that anyone can embark on with the right inspiration.

So, as you read these accounts of curious young minds who later changed the world, know that they aren't just pieces of history. They are blueprints for a brighter future, and it's my privilege to share them with you. Together, let's inspire the next generation of thinkers, dreamers, and innovators.

After sharing these inspiring stories, I want to turn to you, dear parents and readers. We've seen how the childhood curiosity of legends like James Clerk Maxwell and Dr. Vikram Sarabhai led them to change the course of history.

Now, let's think about how we, as parents, educators, and guardians, can nurture that same spark in our children.

Children are born curious. They see the world with wonder and ask questions that make us stop and think. But are we doing enough to fuel that fire of curiosity, or are we unintentionally dampening it by being too focused on rules, routines, and results?

Here are some practical and creative ways to spark curiosity and creativity in your child:

• Hand them crayons and let them colour on something unexpected. How about an old pair of shoes or a piece of cardboard? Breaking away from traditional canvases encourages outside-the-box thinking.

• Give them newspapers or magazines to cut out pictures. Ask them to sort these into categories or make collages that tell a story. This combines creativity with critical thinking.

• Provide clay or playdough. Encourage them to shape objects from their surroundings—perhaps a flower they saw or a favorite toy. It's a hands-on way to learn observation and fine motor skills.

• Let them experiment with safe, unused household materials. Old wires, fabric scraps, or bottle caps can transform into art or even prototypes of their imaginative ideas.

• Sort pulses, grains, or vegetables in fun ways. Ask them to create patterns or "art" on a tray using different colors and textures. This simple activity builds both creativity and concentration.

• Introduce them to nature. A fish tank, a garden, or even caring for a small pet like a bird or turtle can teach responsibility, empathy, and curiosity about life.

• Turn the garage or a storeroom into a workshop. With supervision, let them build using cardboard boxes, packing supplies, or unused tools. Watch their imaginations take flight!

• Encourage messy play in the garden. Digging in the soil, planting seeds, and observing insects provide lessons in science, patience, and the beauty of growth.

• Make the kitchen their lab. With safe tools and ingredients, let them explore cooking, mixing colors, or creating shapes with dough. Everyday surroundings can become magical with the right perspective.

And here's a crucial piece of advice: embrace the mess. A messy home often reflects a mind at work. Let them experiment freely, and teach them to clean up afterward. This not only builds responsibility but also instills pride in their efforts.

The Power of Asking Questions

Encourage their questions, no matter how simple or complex. If they ask, "Why is the sky blue?" turn it into a fun experiment or a shared discovery session. Ask them questions too: "What do you think would happen if…?" or "How would you solve this problem?" This practice will sharpen their critical thinking and make them feel valued.

Why Does This Matter?

The more we nurture curiosity, the less reliant children become on screens for entertainment. They'll find joy in exploring the real world, discovering its wonders, and learning through experience. These moments of discovery will form the foundation for their confidence, creativity, and resilience.

As parents, our role isn't to give all the answers. It's to open doors, spark ideas, and step aside so they can explore. By doing so, we equip them with something far more valuable than information: the love of learning.

So, what will you do today to ignite that spark of curiosity in your child? Perhaps it's as simple as handing them a pair of crayons—or as profound as encouraging their wildest questions. Either way, you're shaping a future filled with wonder and limitless possibilities.

The Mystery of the Moon's Changing Face

It was a calm evening, and Kiara and I were sitting in the living room after dinner. The moonlight streamed through the window, casting soft shadows.

"Papa," Kiara asked, her voice filled with wonder, "why isn't the moon always round? Yesterday, it was bigger, and now it's small again."

I smiled and said, "That's such a great question, Kiara! Let me show you something to help you understand. We're going to solve this mystery together!"

Her eyes lit up with excitement. "Really? How?"

I went to the corner of the room and picked up a ball from her toy basket. Then I grabbed a lamp from the side table and switched it on. "This lamp," I said, "will be the sun. And this ball will be the moon. You'll be the Earth. Ready to see some magic?"

Kiara giggled. "Yes, Papa!"

I placed the ball in her hands and positioned the lamp at eye level. "Now, hold the ball out in front of you and stand still. What do you see?"

She looked closely. "I see the whole ball! It's glowing!"

"Exactly," I said. "That's like a full moon. When the Earth, moon, and sun are in a straight line, we can see the whole moon because the sunlight shines on its face."

"Wow!" she said, her curiosity deepening.

"Now," I continued, "slowly turn your body to the side, but keep holding the ball."

She turned, and her face lit up with surprise. "Papa, I can only see half the ball now!"

"That's right!" I said. "Now we're at the first quarter moon. Only part of the moon is lit up because of where it is in its orbit around the Earth."

Kiara's excitement grew as she kept turning. When she turned further, she gasped. "Papa! The ball is almost dark now!"

I nodded. "That's the new moon. When the moon is between the Earth and the sun, the side facing us isn't lit up. It looks like it disappears, but it's still there."

Her face was full of awe. "So the moon changes because of how the sunlight falls on it?"

"Exactly!" I said, beaming. "The moon doesn't actually change shape—it just looks different from Earth because of how it moves around us."

Kiara stared at the ball, deep in thought. "The moon is like this ball playing hide and seek with the sun!"

I laughed. "That's a great way to think about it! Now, let's make it even more fun. For the next week, why don't you observe the moon every night and draw how it changes? By the end, you'll have your very own moon journal."

Her eyes sparkled with determination. "I'm going to start tonight!" she said, running to grab her notebook and crayons.

Over the next week, Kiara diligently recorded the moon's phases, peppering me with questions like, "Why does the moon move?" and "What makes it go away during the day?" Each answer led her to uncover more mysteries.

One evening, as we reviewed her drawings, she looked up and said, "Papa, I think I solved the mystery! The moon doesn't really change—it just looks different because of the sun!"

"That's absolutely right," I said, giving her a high-five. "And do you know what I love most? The way you observed, asked questions, and figured it out yourself. That's the magic of curiosity, Kiara. When we're curious, we can uncover the secrets of the world."

Her smile stretched ear to ear as she hugged her notebook. "Can we solve another mystery tomorrow, Papa?"

"Of course," I said. "The world is full of mysteries waiting for you to uncover."

By actively involving children in simple experiments and encouraging them to explore and think independently, parents can nurture curiosity and critical thinking. It's not about giving answers—it's about creating opportunities for discovery.

CHAPTER SIX

HomeSchool: Redefining Learning Beyond the Classroom

For generations, parents have believed that learning begins and ends within the walls of a school. They recall their own childhoods, where attending school, completing homework, and preparing for exams felt like the central pillars of education. But is that all education is supposed to be?

We need to rethink this notion. Schools, no matter how well-structured, operate on a standardized curriculum designed to serve the masses. They aim for efficiency, not necessarily deep learning. But children are not identical products rolling off an assembly line—they are individuals with distinct interests, learning styles, and speeds. True learning is not confined to textbooks, report cards, or scheduled lessons; it happens in the everyday moments, in the curiosity sparked by an observation, in the questions that arise during dinner, and in the hands-on experiences that shape a child's understanding of the world.

Homeschooling is a powerful alternative that puts the reins of education back into the hands of parents. It is not merely about replacing a traditional school with a home-based one; rather, it is about embracing a flexible, personalized, and deeply immersive approach to learning—one that adapts to the child rather than forcing the child to adapt to the system.

The Freedom to Learn, The Freedom to Grow

At its core, homeschooling grants parents the ability to craft an educational experience tailored to their child's unique needs. Unlike traditional schooling, where every student must conform to a fixed pace and syllabus, homeschooling allows children to explore subjects at their own rhythm.

Consider a child who is passionate about space. Instead of limiting their learning to a single science period, homeschooling allows parents to design an immersive experience—reading books on astronomy, watching documentaries, building models of planets, and even connecting with experts through online forums. Learning, in this way, becomes an adventure rather than a chore.

This flexibility doesn't just enhance academic learning; it nurtures essential life skills. A child who struggles with math but thrives in creative arts can be taught mathematical concepts through design, architecture, or even music. A child with an entrepreneurial spark can learn financial literacy by setting up a small business project at home. The possibilities are endless when learning is customized rather than standardized.

Lessons from History: The Power of Unconventional Learning

Consider the early life of Albert Einstein.

As a child, Einstein struggled with speech delays, which led many to think he would not excel academically. However, his parents, particularly his mother, supported his natural curiosity. When he developed a fascination with a small compass his father gave him, they encouraged his curiosity rather than dismissing it as childish play. They patiently answered his endless questions and provided resources to deepen his understanding of the world around him.

This nurturing approach helped Einstein develop the ability to focus deeply on problems, a skill that would later define his groundbreaking discoveries in physics. His patience and persistence—qualities instilled through small, meaningful moments during his childhood—became key drivers of his success.

A powerful example comes from the early life of Thomas Edison, one of history's greatest inventors.

As a child, Edison was naturally curious and often bombarded his mother with endless questions about how things worked. One day, young Edison came across a book about chemistry and became fascinated by experiments. Instead of dismissing his curiosity, his mother encouraged him, even allowing him to set up a small lab in their home. However, when Edison's early experiments failed, he didn't give up. His mother patiently guided him to learn from his mistakes, teaching him that perseverance and effort were the keys to success. This foundation of discipline and resilience later helped Edison overcome thousands of failed attempts before finally inventing the light bulb.

As parents, we must take an active role in creating an environment at home where children feel free to explore, experiment, and grow. Home is not just a place to rest after school; it's a child's first laboratory, where the real foundation of their personality is built. Every household is unique, and the environment we create shapes our child's behaviour, thoughts, and future.

One of the key differentiators of homeschooling is its ability to integrate real-world learning into daily life. Traditional schools often isolate subjects into distinct periods, whereas homeschooling fosters interdisciplinary learning.

A simple trip to a grocery store can turn into a lesson on budgeting, nutrition, and even economics.

Time spent in the kitchen can become an exploration of science and mathematics through cooking.

This approach not only enriches the learning experience but also bridges the gap between academic knowledge and practical skills.

While parents put immense effort into choosing the best schools, teachers, and facilities for their children, they sometimes overlook the importance of the home environment. How parents act, speak, and interact within the household has a far greater impact on a child's mind than we realize.

A modern homeschooling setup can be a creative, engaging, and highly personalized experience for both parents and children. By focusing on a child-centered learning approach, parents can tailor the education process to align with their child's unique interests and passions.

For example, if a child is fascinated by animals, parents can integrate biology, nature studies, and animal-related books into their lessons. This approach makes learning feel like an exploration rather than a structured classroom experience, igniting curiosity and fostering a love for learning.

One effective strategy is project-based learning, where children work on projects that combine multiple subjects. A project about building a model of the solar system, for example, can include science, math, and art, teaching the child problem-solving, creativity, and how different disciplines are interconnected. These projects promote hands-on learning, which is crucial for developing cognitive and logical thinking.

The learning environment itself should be flexible and stimulating. Creating different "learning zones" in the home for reading, art, and experiments allows the child to move between spaces based on their interests. These zones should be filled with vibrant colors, educational tools, and sensory objects to keep the child engaged without overwhelming them. The space should feel like a place of discovery, not a traditional classroom.

Incorporating technology can also be a valuable tool in modern homeschooling. Using interactive educational apps, websites, and self-paced platforms like Khan Academy or Duolingo gives children the autonomy to explore subjects they're interested in, all while developing problem-solving skills. These resources can be used at the child's own pace, further promoting independence in learning.

To ensure productivity and prevent distractions, parents can use visual schedules, timers for focused work sessions, and regular breaks. This structure helps children understand the flow of their day, giving them the autonomy to engage in self-directed learning while maintaining some consistency. For cognitive and logical development, introducing critical thinking challenges like puzzles, riddles, or simple science experiments encourages children to reason, hypothesize, and test their ideas.

Parents can also play a collaborative role by setting clear goals, but leaving room for children to direct their own learning. This approach not only allows for creative exploration but also gives children the freedom to learn without constant supervision. Weekly check-ins can provide opportunities for reflection and discussion, giving parents a chance to gauge progress and adjust as necessary.

Furthermore, integrating real-life experiences, such as cooking, gardening, or managing money, into learning helps children see the practical applications of their education. These activities promote life skills and make learning feel meaningful and connected to the world around them. Socialization can be facilitated through homeschool co-ops, group projects, or virtual learning groups, allowing children to collaborate and develop communication skills.

Finally, this modern homeschooling system should evolve with the child's needs, ensuring that the learning process remains dynamic and suited to their growth. By allowing the child to take the lead in their education, parents foster a sense of ownership over their learning, encouraging a deeper, more intrinsic motivation to continue exploring, discovering, and growing.

This approach combines creativity, autonomy, and logical thinking, ensuring that the child's learning experience is both engaging and meaningful. The flexibility of this system ensures that it doesn't feel like a conventional school setup, providing the child with the freedom to learn in a way that suits their individual pace and interests.

KEY TAKEAWAYS :

1. Turn Daily Activities into Lessons

• Grocery Shopping → A Math & Budgeting Lesson

→ Let your child compare prices, estimate totals, or count change.

• Cooking → Science & Chemistry

→ Talk about how baking soda makes bread rise or how oil and water don't mix.

• Gardening → Biology & Responsibility

→ Teach patience by growing a plant together and observing changes daily.

These simple moments bridge academics with real life—something schools often struggle to do.

2. Create Learning Zones at Home

Children learn best when their space inspires them. Set up different learning areas:

• A "creation station" for drawing, puzzles, or crafts.

• A cozy reading nook filled with age-appropriate books.

• A hands-on experiment corner for exploring science through play.

No need for fancy setups—just declutter, organize, and make learning accessible.

3. Use Technology the Right Way

Instead of banning screens altogether, use them wisely:

• Apps like Khan Academy Kids, Duolingo, or Tynker turn screen time into valuable learning.

• Audiobooks and podcasts make car rides educational.

• YouTube can be a great tool—just curate what they watch (think science experiments, storytelling, or history animations).

Screens shouldn't replace interaction but can enhance learning when used intentionally.

The "Unsaid Curriculum" – What Your Child Learns Without You Realizing

Every action, every word, and even every unspoken gesture you make as a parent or teacher profoundly influences the way a child thinks, feels, and behaves. Children are not just passive recipients of information—they absorb the essence of the environment around them, forming their worldviews based on what they observe. These observations shape their understanding of emotions, relationships, and how they interact with the world. It's crucial to recognize that children often learn more from what they witness than from what we directly teach them. This subtle but powerful form of learning—what might be called the "unsaid curriculum"—is equally, if not more, important than explicit instruction.

As parents and teachers, we are the architects of this "unsaid curriculum." We teach through our actions, choices, and attitudes, and the way we respond to daily situations. The tone we use when we speak, our reactions in moments of stress, the values we model in our interactions—all of these things leave a lasting imprint on a child's mind. Even the smallest of daily habits—whether we express gratitude, whether we react to challenges calmly or with frustration—helps a child develop an emotional framework that they will carry with them into adulthood.

Take a moment to reflect on the following questions:

• How do you handle conflicts at home?

Children are watching how we resolve disagreements and challenges. If they see parents managing conflict with respect, patience, and understanding, they internalize these behaviors as effective strategies for resolving their own disputes. But if conflict is handled with shouting, avoidance, or aggression, they may learn that such methods are acceptable.

• How do you treat people around you?

Whether it's the delivery person, a helper, or a neighbor, children observe how we treat others. If we show kindness, respect, and empathy toward everyone, regardless of their role or status, we are teaching our children to do the same. On the other hand, if we display rudeness or indifference, that becomes the unspoken lesson they learn.

• How do you react when plans go wrong?

Life is unpredictable, and things often don't go according to plan. How we handle these moments—whether we remain calm and adaptable or become upset and reactive—teaches our children how to navigate their own frustrations. This resilience in the face of disappointment is a valuable skill that shapes their ability to cope with challenges throughout life.

• How much time do you spend on your devices?

In today's world, digital devices are often a distraction, and if a child observes constant phone checking or excessive screen time, they may learn that this is the norm. However, if we prioritize quality time with them, set boundaries around device use, and engage in meaningful conversations, it helps reinforce the importance of presence and connection over distractions.

• Are you expressing gratitude or dissatisfaction?

Gratitude is a powerful lesson. If we regularly express gratitude for what we have—whether it's for the food on our table, the relationships we cherish, or the small blessings of daily life—children learn to appreciate the present and develop a positive mindset. On the other hand, if we constantly voice dissatisfaction or focus on what's missing, children may internalize feelings of scarcity or entitlement.

Children's subconscious minds are like sponges—they absorb and process everything. They are not only learning from what is taught explicitly but also from what is left unspoken. When we as parents and educators become more mindful of our words, actions, and the environment we create, we provide children with a foundation for emotional intelligence, empathy, and resilience. This process is not about perfection but about striving to be aware of the example we set, because our children will inevitably mirror what they observe.

The environment at home plays a pivotal role in shaping a child's mental and emotional framework. A serene, peaceful atmosphere provides the emotional safety children need to thrive. When the home is calm, filled with understanding, patience, and respect, it fosters a sense of security that allows children to explore their interests, express themselves freely, and grow with confidence. A home environment that reflects positive energy not only nurtures the child's emotional well-being but also supports their cognitive development.

In addition to creating this nurturing atmosphere, it's also essential to acknowledge how children's minds process information. The subconscious mind, especially in early childhood, is highly impressionable. Stress, anxiety, and negative energy at home can leave deep imprints on their subconscious, affecting their self-esteem, emotional regulation, and social skills. Conversely, a calm, loving, and nurturing environment provides the child with a sense of stability and balance. When children feel emotionally safe, they are more open to learning, more willing to explore new ideas, and better equipped to face challenges.

Moreover, children thrive in environments that encourage not just academic growth, but emotional growth as well. This is where the power of homeschooling becomes even more significant. While homeschooling offers the flexibility to design a curriculum based on a child's interests and needs, it's equally important to integrate emotional learning into the structure. The serenity of the home environment, combined with purposeful, child-centered education, creates a holistic approach to their development.

As parents and educators, we have the power to create this ideal environment. It's not about creating a perfect space, but about being mindful of our actions, our attitudes, and the energy we bring into the home. When we set this foundation of calm, empathy, and emotional intelligence, we not only support the academic development of the child but also nurture their emotional strength, self-awareness, and capacity for compassion.

Creating a serene and mindful home environment is more than just an ideal; it is a fundamental pillar for raising well-rounded, emotionally resilient, and compassionate children.

KEY TAKEAWAYS

? Encourage Self-Directed Learning

Give kids choices in their learning. Let them pick books, projects, or activities—it boosts ownership and motivation.

? Incorporate Life Skills

Let them help with finances, household management, or even simple decision-making. These are critical lessons schools often miss.

? Foster a Growth Mindset

Praise effort, not just results. Teach kids that mistakes are stepping stones, not failures.

? Prioritize Emotional Intelligence

Teach children to name their feelings, practice empathy, and navigate conflicts. Emotional intelligence predicts success more than IQ.

✔ Every child is unique—learning should reflect that. Traditional school isn't enough; home learning fills the gaps.

✓ Daily life is a classroom. Small moments—like cooking or shopping—hold powerful lessons.

✓ Your behavior is the first curriculum. Kids don't just listen to what you say; they absorb what you do.

✓ Balance structured learning with real-world experiences. Life skills matter as much as academics.

✓ Homeschooling doesn't mean replacing school. It means making home an active place for growth, curiosity, and lifelong learning.

CHAPTER SEVEN

The Art of Storytelling

It was a late Sunday afternoon, one of those rare days when my wife and I were both home with no pressing deadlines or calls to attend. Our younger daughter, Kyna, was napping, and our older daughter, Kiara, was playing in the living room. The air felt calm, but what unfolded next shook me to my core and left me questioning my approach as a parent.

I was sitting on the couch scrolling through my phone, reading emails and catching up on messages, while my wife was busy preparing tea in the kitchen. Kiara, with her boundless energy, had been flitting around the house all morning. That's when I noticed her, crouched near the electrical outlet, her little fingers curiously prodding at the switchboard. My heart skipped a beat.

"Kiara! Stop that right now!" I snapped. The sharpness of my voice startled her, and she froze, looking at me with wide, innocent eyes. My wife rushed out of the kitchen, alarmed by my tone, and immediately joined in.

"You know better than to play with those switches!" my wife scolded, picking her up and moving her away from the outlet. Kiara's face crumpled, and tears began streaming down her cheeks. She wasn't crying out of guilt or defiance—it was the confusion and hurt of being misunderstood.

For a moment, the room was silent except for her quiet sobs. I looked at my phone in my hand, then at Kiara's tear-streaked face, and a wave of guilt washed over me. Why was she playing near the switchboard? Was it really "mischief," or was she simply exploring her world in the only way a curious 4-year-old knows how?

I sat down beside her on the floor and gently pulled her into my lap. "Kiara, were you curious about how the switches work?" I asked softly. She nodded, still sniffling, and buried her face in my chest. My wife, who had been watching, sighed and sat next to us.

"I think we scared her more than we protected her," I admitted. My wife nodded, and we both knew this wasn't about the switchboard anymore—it was about the way we were parenting.

That night, after the girls went to bed, my wife and I had a long conversation. We realized how often we had been distracted—me with my phone, her with household chores—while Kiara played by herself. She wasn't being mischievous; she was simply exploring the world around her because we weren't there to guide her curiosity.

The harsh truth hit us like a ton of bricks: we had unintentionally created an environment where Kiara was left to navigate her curiosity alone. And worse, when she did explore, we reprimanded her instead of nurturing her curiosity in a safe, constructive way.

The very next weekend, we decided to dedicate a day completely to Kiara. We left our phones in the bedroom and planned simple activities she could enjoy with us. We planted a small flower pot in the balcony together, explaining how plants grow. Kiara was ecstatic, carefully sprinkling soil and seeds with her tiny hands. She named the plant "Rosy" and declared she would water it every day.

Later, we sat with her and made a small scrapbook using petals she had collected during our last visit to the park. As we cut and pasted, she chatted endlessly about the colors and shapes, her laughter filling the room. For the first time in weeks, I felt fully present—not just physically, but emotionally, too.

This incident taught us an important lesson: children don't act out of defiance; they act out of curiosity. It's our responsibility as parents to guide that curiosity, not suppress it. Scolding or handing over a screen might provide a temporary fix, but it doesn't address their deeper need for connection, understanding, and learning.

In today's world, where work demands are high, and extended family support is rare, it's easy to let screens replace meaningful interactions. But at what cost? Children remember moments spent together—laughter, shared activities, and the feeling of being seen and valued—not the gadgets they owned.

As I reflect on that day, I realize this isn't just my story. It's the story of countless parents struggling to balance responsibilities and meaningful engagement with their children. If we continue to rely on screens to fill the gaps, we risk losing the most precious gift we can give our children: our presence.

So, the next time your child fumbles with switches, scribbles on walls, or dismantles a toy, pause. Instead of reacting with frustration, sit down with them. Ask questions. Be curious with them. Because every moment you invest today will shape the way they view the world—and you—for the rest of their lives.

It's essential to recognize that you hold the key to reshaping this narrative. While the world around us has changed, your responsibility as a parent remains timeless: to nurture, guide, and support your child's growth. Your child's experiences today will shape the person they become tomorrow. The values, memories, and lessons they carry into adulthood depend on how you approach their childhood.

History and the lives of great achievers show us how profoundly childhood experiences and parenting influence a person's trajectory. Steve Jobs, the co-founder of Apple, often credited his adoptive parents for fostering his creative spark and curiosity. He once shared how his father's meticulous carpentry work inspired him to value craftsmanship, even in areas people wouldn't see. This early lesson laid the foundation for his perfectionist approach to design and innovation.

Similarly, Nobel laureate Malala Yousafzai has spoken about how her father's unwavering belief in her abilities gave her the courage to fight for education rights. Despite societal norms in her community, her father stood firm, encouraging her to dream big and pursue her passion. She often attributes her confidence and resilience to the love and support she received from her family.

In another example, Mahatma Gandhi, one of the most influential leaders in history, often reminisced about the moral lessons his mother instilled in him during his childhood. Her steadfast devotion to truth and compassion became the guiding principles of his life and his philosophy of nonviolent resistance, which changed the course of history.

Even Albert Einstein, whose name is synonymous with genius, credited his parents for nurturing his innate curiosity. His mother's encouragement to play the violin and his father's gift of a compass ignited a lifelong fascination with the mysteries of the universe. These small acts of thoughtful parenting planted the seeds for his revolutionary discoveries.

These examples are a powerful reminder that greatness often begins with small, consistent acts of guidance and love. As a parent, you are shaping not just your child's future but their entire worldview. By being present, fostering curiosity, and instilling values like empathy, resilience, and integrity, you are building the foundation for their success—both personal and professional.

Think about it: the warmth of your encouragement during their small victories, the patience with which you guide them through their failures, and the memories of shared laughter and learning will stay with them forever. These moments will not only form their emotional core but also give them the confidence to navigate life's challenges.

Parenting is not about creating perfection but about nurturing potential. When you look at the stories of great individuals, their successes are rarely the result of isolated genius. Instead, they are a cumulative effect of consistent love, support, and lessons from their formative years. The effort you put into your child today might not yield immediate results, but rest assured, it will echo in their lives for years to come.

Your role in your child's life is timeless and irreplaceable. So, every time you engage with your child, remember: you are not just raising a child—you are shaping a legacy. The world they build tomorrow will reflect the care, guidance, and love you invest in them today.

Building a meaningful, screen-free childhood requires intentional effort. It means stepping away from your distractions, understanding your child's needs, and creating opportunities for connection and growth. The time and attention you invest in your child are not just acts of care—they are a foundation for their future and a reflection of your commitment to their well-being.

This is not just a task but a profound responsibility. Embracing it wholeheartedly can transform not only your child's life but also your relationship with them. When you take the time to truly understand your child's world and actively participate in it, you're not just guiding them—you're building a legacy of love, trust, and shared joy that will last a lifetime.

Here Are the Little Things That Can Make a Huge Difference

Engaging your child doesn't require grand gestures; small, thoughtful actions can create a profound impact. One of the simplest ways is to involve your child in whatever activity you're doing. For example, if you're cooking, invite them to join you. At first, it might feel chaotic as they explore and put their hands on everything. But with patience and gentle guidance, they will begin to understand what to do, when to do it, and how they can genuinely help.

This process isn't just about teaching them skills—it's about fostering connection. While they're involved, take the opportunity to converse with them. Share stories from your childhood: the first time you cooked, the mistakes you made, or a funny memory related to that task. Don't just narrate facts; weave a story. Add a touch of imagination, a dash of humour, and a sprinkle of mystery to keep them engaged.

For instance, instead of simply saying, "I learned cooking when I was 10," create a vivid story: "When I was 10, I tried to make tea for the first time, but instead of sugar, I added salt! Everyone laughed, but I learned an important lesson about paying attention."

Build these stories with care. Include little fictional elements, relatable challenges, and subtle moral values. Don't overwhelm the story with lessons; let the values flow naturally, like a hidden gem your child discovers on their own. Add twists and turns, create suspense, and leave them eagerly waiting to hear what happens next.

Let me give you an example about one such incident I have shared with my daughter.

The Day I Saved the Little Bird

"Kiara," I said, settling her into bed, "did I ever tell you about the time I became a hero for a day?"

Her eyes widened, and she shook her head eagerly. "What happened, Papa?"

"Well, when I was about your age, I loved playing in the backyard of our old house. There was a huge guava tree, its branches so thick with leaves that it felt like a jungle. I would spend hours pretending I was an adventurer, discovering hidden treasures or fighting imaginary dragons. One day, while I was climbing the tree, I heard a tiny sound—a soft chirp that didn't sound quite right."

Kiara interrupted, "Was it a bird?"

"Yes," I said with a grin. "I looked around and saw a tiny baby bird, no bigger than my hand, lying on the ground. Its wing was hurt, and it couldn't fly. It looked up at me with its small, frightened eyes, as if asking for help. My first thought was to call someone else—maybe Grandpa—but then I remembered the stories Grandpa used to tell me about being brave and helping those in need."

"What did you do?" she asked, her voice filled with concern.

"I decided to be brave and help the little bird myself," I continued. "I tore a piece of cloth from an old shirt I had brought to the backyard for my adventures and gently wrapped the bird to keep it warm. Then I climbed down the tree very carefully, one hand holding the bird and the other gripping the branches. My heart was beating so fast—what if I fell? But I kept reminding myself: 'The little bird is counting on me.' That gave me the courage to keep going."

Kiara's eyes lit up. "You were like a superhero!"

"Exactly!" I chuckled. "Once I was safely on the ground, I made a small nest using some soft grass and placed the bird inside. I remembered Grandpa saying that every creature deserves kindness, so I brought the bird some water in a bottle cap and tiny bits of fruit. Over the next few days, I kept checking on it, making sure it was safe and cared for. I even built a small shelter from sticks to protect it from the rain."

"Did the bird get better?" Kiara asked, leaning forward.

"Yes," I said, nodding. "After about a week, I saw it flutter its wings. Slowly but surely, it started to hop and then fly short distances. One morning, it flew all the way to the top of the guava tree and chirped so loudly, as if it was saying thank you. I felt so proud—not because I saved a bird, but because I overcame my fear and helped someone who couldn't help themselves."

Kiara beamed. "You were really brave, Papa! And kind too!"

"That's the lesson, Kiara," I said, stroking her hair. "Being brave doesn't mean you're not afraid. It means you do the right thing, even when you are. And being kind to others—no matter how small or big they are—makes the world a better place."

As she drifted off to sleep, I felt a warm sense of satisfaction, knowing that the story of my childhood had planted another seed of courage and empathy in her little heart.

Take this as an opportunity to introduce your child to the characters from your own life—your parents, your siblings, your friends. Let them imagine your childhood: the games you played, the mistakes you made, the love and care you received. These stories are not just entertaining—they create a bridge between generations, instilling a deep sense of belonging, love, and gratitude in your child.

When your child sees you cherish and respect your parents and siblings, they begin to develop similar feelings of gratitude for their family. This simple act of sharing your life stories not only strengthens your bond but also shapes your child's understanding of relationships and values in a natural, joyful way.

Remember, it's the little things—like inviting them into your world and sharing a piece of your history—that can leave the deepest, most lasting impression.

Arrogance

How do parents unknowingly raise little emperors who rule over arrogance?

The Problem: The Crown that Doesn't Fit

Imagine this: A child is at a birthday party playing a game, but they lose to another kid. Instead of learning to handle the disappointment, the child throws a tantrum, shouting that the game was "unfair."

The parent steps in, soothing the child by blaming the game's rules or even the other children, saying, "You were the real winner; they just don't know how great you are." The other parents and children are left bewildered, but the child walks away feeling like royalty whose word is law.

This pattern—where parents constantly cover for their children, shield them from failure, and validate bad behavior—lays the groundwork for a life of arrogance and entitlement. Children raised this way grow up believing they're beyond reproach, leading to difficulty in forming healthy relationships, working in teams, or handling criticism.

The Roots of Arrogance

This princely feeling doesn't grow in isolation. It's often nurtured by:

1. Overpraise Without Merit

Every scribble becomes a masterpiece, every misstep a "learning style," and every failed test is dismissed with, "It's not your fault; the teacher is just bad at explaining."

• Impact: The child begins to believe they are above correction and that effort is optional because perfection is their birthright.

2. Parents Playing the Blame Game

Teachers, friends, relatives—everyone becomes a scapegoat when something goes wrong. "You didn't do well in sports day? It's because the coach doesn't know your potential."

• Impact: The child learns to externalize blame and never takes responsibility for their actions.

3. The Bubble of Superiority

Some parents, often unknowingly, inflate their child's ego by comparing them to others: "Look how much better you are than your classmates."

• Impact: This comparison fosters a false sense of superiority, creating a child who looks down on others.

4. Misplaced Parental Pride

Parents often see their child as an extension of themselves. Critiquing the child feels like critiquing their own parenting. To protect their image, they shield the child from accountability.

• Impact: The child misses out on learning essential lessons like humility and self-improvement.

Real-Life Scenarios: Arrogance in the Making

1. The Sports Showdown

A child loses a football match but refuses to shake hands with the winning team. Instead of addressing this unsportsmanlike behavior, the parent consoles the child by saying, "It's not your fault; the referee was biased."

• Result: The child learns to deflect failure onto others and avoids building resilience.

2. The Restaurant Meltdown

At a family dinner, a child throws a fit because their favorite dessert isn't available. The parent immediately calls over the staff, demanding they "figure something out" because "my child deserves the best."

• Result: The child begins to believe that their desires are more important than everyone else's, leading to entitlement.

3. The Birthday Party Incident

A child snatches a toy from another child at a birthday party. When confronted by the host, the parent laughs it off, saying, "Oh, they're just assertive! Isn't it cute?"

• Result: The child learns to justify selfish behavior and expects others to excuse their actions.

4. The Report Card Excuse

A child gets poor grades, but instead of encouraging improvement, the parent criticizes the teacher and school system: "They don't recognize your potential."

• Result: The child avoids self-reflection and begins to think their shortcomings are always someone else's fault.

5. The Group Project Conflict

During a school project, a child refuses to collaborate with teammates and dominates all decisions. When the teacher brings this up, the parent responds with, "My child is just a natural leader; maybe the other kids aren't pulling their weight."

• Result: The child becomes difficult to work with and alienates peers.

Right Now, You Have the Power to Shape Your Child's Character—Don't Miss This Life-Changing Opportunity

Parenting is more than just providing love and care—it's about shaping the person your child will become. Right now, you have an incredible opportunity to raise a kind, confident, and humble human being. The way you respond to their actions today will determine whether they grow into a compassionate leader or an entitled individual.

Arrogance doesn't develop overnight—it's a result of repeated patterns, unchecked behaviors, and missed chances to teach valuable lessons. But here's the good news: you have the power to break the cycle, starting now. Every moment is an opportunity to guide your child toward humility, kindness, and genuine self-worth.

10 Life-Changing Shifts to Raise a Grounded, Empathetic Child

1. Shift from "You're So Smart" to "You Worked Hard"

Instead of feeding their ego with fixed praise, help them build a growth mindset. When they solve a puzzle, say, "You kept trying even when it was tough—I love that!" instead of, "You're a genius!" This teaches them to value perseverance over praise.

➡ Make it Count: Ask, "What was the hardest part, and how did you overcome it?" This turns every challenge into a moment of self-reflection.

2. Stop Making Excuses—Teach Accountability Instead

The next time your child is rude or careless, don't brush it off as "just a phase." Instead, make them responsible for fixing it. When they hurt a friend's feelings, ask, "How do you think they felt?" and encourage them to apologize.

➡ Make it Count: Say, "Mistakes are okay, but what's important is making things right. How can we fix this together?" This builds lifelong integrity.

3. Replace "Be Nice" with Real Empathy

Instead of forcing kindness, make them feel it. If they refuse to share, ask, "How would you feel if your friend did this to you?" Helping them see the world from others' eyes reduces arrogance.

➡ Make it Count: Role-play situations—"What if you were the teacher and no one listened to you?" This makes empathy real.

4. Be the Example—Show, Don't Tell

Your child is always watching. If you blame others for mistakes, they will too. But if they see you say, "Oops, I forgot my keys—that was my mistake," they'll learn to own up to their actions.

➡ Make it Count: Share your own learning moments. "I once failed a test because I didn't study enough. That mistake taught me to plan better." This shows that everyone has room to grow.

5. Eliminate Comparison—Focus on Their Growth

Telling your child they're "the best" only builds arrogance. Instead of saying, "You're smarter than others," say, "You've improved so much since last time!"

➡ Make it Count: Help them set personal goals: "Last month, you read two books. Let's try for three this month!" This makes success about growth, not superiority.

6. Let Consequences Do the Teaching

If they forget their homework, don't rescue them. If they're rude, let them experience the social fallout. Protecting them from discomfort teaches entitlement.

➡ Make it Count: Instead of scolding, ask, "What did you learn from this?" When they find their own solutions, the lesson sticks.

7. Don't Inflate Their Ego—Balance Praise with Growth

Praising your child for every small thing can make them expect constant validation. Instead of saying, "You're perfect," say, "You did great, and here's one way you can get even better!"

➡ Make it Count: Use the compliment sandwich: Praise → Constructive feedback → Encouragement. "Your drawing is so creative! Let's work on coloring inside the lines next time. I know you'll get even better!"

8. Shift from "Giving" to "Earning"

When children get everything they want without effort, they start expecting it. Teach them that privileges come with responsibility.

➡ Make it Count: Create a reward system where they earn points for kindness, chores, or responsibility. This makes them appreciate what they receive.

9. Make Gratitude a Daily Habit

A grateful child is a humble child. Before meals, ask everyone to share one thing they're thankful for.

➡ Make it Count: Encourage them to write thank-you notes or volunteer as a family. Seeing the world beyond themselves fosters humility.

10. Be the Parent, Not the Protector of Pride

It's tempting to shield your child from discomfort or correction, but true growth comes from learning to handle feedback.

➡ Make it Count: Teach them that corrections = learning. Say, "Even I get corrected sometimes—it helps me improve." This builds resilience.

Right Now, You Are Creating the Person Your Child Will Become

Every choice you make—every word, every response—shapes your child's character. The opportunity to raise a kind, humble, and strong human is in your hands today.

If you wait until arrogance has already taken root, undoing it will be much harder. But if you start making small, intentional shifts today, you will see a remarkable transformation.

Don't wait. Start now. Your child's future depends on it.

A Reminder for Parents

Parenting isn't about creating a flawless child; it's about raising a thoughtful, empathetic, and humble individual. Your child will make mistakes—it's inevitable. What matters is how you guide them to learn, grow, and thrive in the real world.

CHAPTER NINE

The Role Reversal Technique

When Dreams Crumble: The Test of Parenting Amidst Failure

TWO YEAR AGO,

I embarked on what I believed was my life's defining project—the dream of building my own school. It wasn't just a business idea; it was a vision I had nurtured for years. A place where education wouldn't just be about textbooks and exams but about shaping young minds with curiosity and purpose. I imagined classrooms filled with creativity, discussions that sparked real thinking, and an environment that felt more like a second home than an institution.

For 12 months, I lived and breathed this project. Every spare moment, every ounce of energy was poured into bringing this dream to life. I meticulously designed the building, ensuring every space would inspire learning. I drafted a curriculum that reflected my belief in meaningful education. I worked on a unique selling point—something that would set my school apart, something parents and children would love. And then, of course, there was the marketing—the strategy that would introduce this dream to the world and make it a reality.

At times, I would lie awake at night, running numbers in my head, tweaking plans, and visualizing the grand opening. I could already hear the laughter of children in the hallways, the sound of eager minds at work. It felt real. It felt inevitable.

And then came the investor meeting.

I walked in with confidence, carrying not just a business proposal but a piece of my soul. I presented everything—my research, my projections, the impact this school could have. I believed in it with every fiber of my being.

But belief alone wasn't enough.

The investor, after listening carefully, shook his head. The numbers didn't work. Land costs were too high. Construction costs were even higher.

The financials didn't align with what they were willing to risk. No matter how much I tried to explain the long-term vision, it came down to one word: No.

I walked out of that meeting with a forced smile, but inside, something shattered. My partner and I tried to salvage what we could, looking for alternatives, brainstorming ways to keep the project alive. But reality was staring us in the face—the dream, as we had envisioned it, was not going to happen.

Eventually, after exhausting every possibility, we made the heartbreaking decision to shut it down.

I had spent a year building something that never came to life. Twelve months of relentless effort, gone in a single decision.

Failure isn't just about losing money or time—it's about losing a piece of yourself.

For weeks, I felt hollow. I carried this invisible weight on my shoulders—the crushing disappointment, the unanswered "what ifs," the fear of being seen as someone who couldn't make it work.

But life doesn't pause for heartbreak.

At home, my daughters were still laughing, playing, calling out to me to join them. My four-year-old still asked for bedtime stories. My younger one still reached out for me with her tiny hands, unaware that I was struggling to keep myself together.

And that's when I realized: Failure is one thing. Letting failure steal your presence as a parent is another.

I had two choices—sink into self-pity or show my daughters what resilience looks like.

Rebuilding from Within

Parenting advice often sounds simple: follow these tips, practice these strategies, and everything will fall into place. But when you're in the thick of it, it's not that easy. The frustration of seeing my efforts unravel in one project left me feeling defeated and irritable, and I struggled to cope with the pressures that piled up from work, life, and now the failure of this dream.

There were moments when my children would act out, throw tantrums, or refuse to listen to the simplest requests, and I found myself growing angrier, more impatient, and less understanding. Despite all the parenting books and advice I had absorbed, in those moments of defiance, I couldn't help but question my ability to be a good parent. Why wasn't my effort enough? Why couldn't I understand what my children needed in those moments?

The weight of everything—the work pressures, the failure of the school project, the growing frustration—made it hard to focus on what mattered most. The emotional exhaustion left me feeling like I was building a beautiful sandcastle only for it to be washed away by a sudden tide. I found myself with no strength left to rebuild, and the feelings of helplessness were overwhelming.

But this journey of failure taught me a lot about the importance of perseverance, and even more about the need to be kind to myself. No matter how much effort we put in, things don't always go according to plan—and that's okay.

More importantly, it made me realize how much of our own struggles can affect the way we parent. The key is not to let those moments of failure define us but to keep learning and growing—just as we hope our children will.

The Role Reversal Technique: A Game Changer

In the midst of my struggle, I stumbled upon something that transformed my approach to parenting: The Role Reversal Technique.

Instead of seeing my children's mischief as a problem to fix, I asked myself, What would happen if I joined in? What if, instead of trying to manage the chaos, I added a bit of playful chaos myself?

So, when their antics spilled over into a mess, I laughed with them, embraced their joy, and created shared memories that went beyond discipline. What I had once seen as mischief was really just an overflow of energy or a need for attention.

Rather than reacting with frustration, I became part of the solution. I could offer guidance, but in a way that was aligned with their emotions, without feeling like I had to control every situation.

This shift in perspective brought me closer to my children and allowed me to find peace in my role as a parent. The playful chaos became a way for us to bond, to communicate, and to share in the beauty of childhood, which I realized I had been missing.

Letting Go: The Power of Surrender

But there were still moments—many moments—when everything felt completely out of control. The failures of the past haunted me, the pressures of life stacked up—work, family, finances. It all became overwhelming.

That's when I realized: Life is unpredictable, and no matter how much effort I put in, not every plan will unfold the way I envision it.

I had two choices: live in constant resistance, trying to force everything into place, or surrender to the flow of life.

Surrendering didn't mean giving up. It meant releasing the emotional tension of resistance and trusting that things would unfold as they were meant to. It meant recognizing that while I could influence my circumstances, I couldn't control everything—and I didn't have to.

By embracing this surrender, I created a sense of harmony between my inner world and the outer chaos. It didn't make life perfect, but it allowed me to approach challenges with a calm composure. And that serenity had a powerful effect on how I parented.

Instead of reacting from a place of anxiety or frustration, I could approach my children's energy and emotions with more patience, creativity, and understanding.

The Journey Forward

Parenting isn't about being perfect. It's about navigating the uncertainties of life together, learning and growing alongside our children.

And in that shared experience—the ability to step into their world and allow them into ours—lies the true beauty of parenting.

Through these lessons, I began to realize that even in moments of hardship, there's an opportunity to connect, to bond, and to grow.

Because at the end of the day, parenting isn't about getting everything right.

It's about being present for the moments that matter.

6 Practical Steps to Master the Role Reversal Technique in Parenting

The Role Reversal Technique is a powerful way to shift from controlling your child's behavior to truly understanding it. It allows you to step into their world, see things from their perspective, and build a stronger bond while making discipline more effective. Here's how you can start using it today:

1. Become the Child for 10 Minutes a Day

What to do: Every day, set aside 10 minutes where you completely step into your child's shoes. Join their world without directing or correcting them. If they're playing, play at their level. If they're pretending to be a superhero, be the sidekick.

Why it works: This helps you understand their emotions, thinking process, and what truly excites them. It also strengthens your connection because they see you as someone who values their world.

Try this today: Next time your child plays, instead of saying "Be careful" or "Do it this way", say "Show me how to do it like you!" and follow their lead.

2. Switch Roles During Tough Moments

What to do: When your child is upset, instead of immediately reacting, ask them, "If you were the parent right now, what would you say to help me understand how you feel?"

Why it works: It forces them to articulate their emotions and helps you see their struggle in a way you might have overlooked. It also teaches them empathy by imagining themselves in your position.

Try this today: The next time your child refuses to listen, ask, "If I were you and you were me, what would you say?" Then, let them answer and respond based on their input.

3. Say "YES" to One Unexpected Thing Each Day

What to do: Every day, say YES to one fun or silly thing you'd usually say no to. If they ask to have a picnic on the floor, say yes. If they want you to chase them around the house, go for it.

Why it works: It makes your child feel heard and valued, while also helping you embrace their energy rather than resist it. This creates a more joyful home environment where both parent and child feel connected.

Try this today: When your child asks for something playful, take a deep breath, pause, and say, "Why not?" instead of "Not now."

4. Let Them "Be the Boss" for a Short Time

What to do: Give your child a short period (10-15 minutes) where they get to be in charge. They decide the activity, and you follow their instructions without interference.

Why it works: It builds their confidence and makes them feel respected. It also gives you insight into how they think, what they enjoy, and how they process the world.

Try this today: Say, "For the next 10 minutes, you are the boss! What should we do?" and let them lead.

5. Turn "No" into a Playful Challenge

What to do: Instead of saying "No, you can't do that", turn it into a fun challenge. For example, if they're running around wildly before bedtime, instead of saying "Stop running!", try "Let's see if you can tiptoe like a ninja all the way to bed!"

Why it works: Children respond better to play than to commands. Turning redirection into a game helps them listen without feeling controlled, making parenting smoother and more enjoyable.

Try this today: The next time you're about to say "No" or "Stop", pause and think: How can I turn this into a fun challenge instead?

6. Use "Mistake Moments" to Teach, Not Scold

What to do: When your child makes a mistake, instead of scolding, pretend to be confused and ask for their advice. Say, "Oh no! What should we do now?" and let them come up with a solution.

Why it works: It shifts the focus from blame to problem-solving, helping your child learn responsibility in a positive way. It also makes discipline feel less like punishment and more like teamwork.

Try this today: The next time your child spills something, instead of reacting with frustration, say "Oops! What's the best way to clean this up?" and let them take the lead.

Final Thoughts

Parenting isn't about control—it's about connection. By stepping into your child's world, even for a few moments each day, you build a foundation of trust, joy, and cooperation.

Try one of these steps today and see the difference in how your child responds. The more you practice, the more natural it will become, making parenting not just easier—but more fun for both of you!

CHAPTER TEN

Learn a New Skill

Reignite the Joy of Discovery

As we grow older, something curious happens—we begin to hesitate before learning something new. We don't admit it outright, but our minds start whispering doubts: "Will this be useful? What's the point? Am I too old for this?" Instead of embracing learning for the sake of curiosity, we measure it against a profit-and-loss mindset. "If this won't directly benefit my career, finances, or social status, why bother?"

But let's pause for a moment. Think back to your childhood.

Remember the thrill of picking up a pencil and attempting to sketch your first cartoon character? Or the way your heart raced when you finally balanced on a bicycle for the first time? There was no strategy, no long-term benefit in mind—just the sheer joy of figuring something out.

Why did we stop?

Over time, as responsibilities piled up, we became more rigid. We traded curiosity for routine, passion for predictability, and somewhere along the way, learning became a chore rather than a delight. But here's the truth—our brains are wired to crave new experiences. Every time we challenge ourselves with something unfamiliar, we trigger a surge of dopamine, the brain's feel-good chemical. New skills create new neural connections, keeping our minds sharper, younger, and more adaptable.

But what if we didn't embark on this journey alone?

The Power of Learning With Your Child

Imagine this:

You've never played the flute before. One day, you bring home two flutes—one for you, one for your child. You sit together, fumble through the first few notes, and laugh at the awkward sounds you produce. The journey isn't about mastering the flute overnight. It's about standing at the same starting line as your child, feeling the excitement of the unknown together.

You both watch tutorials, practice, make mistakes, and celebrate small victories—and in doing so, something magical happens. You're no longer just teaching your child; you're experiencing growth alongside them. The shared moments of frustration, perseverance, and triumph build a bond stronger than words.

And it doesn't have to be the flute. The skill itself doesn't matter as much as the shared experience of learning together.

Choosing Your Adventure: Skills to Explore Together

Pick something you've always wanted to try, something you wish you had learned as a child. The beauty of this approach is that there's no pressure to be perfect—just the joy of learning for learning's sake.

1. Musical Instrument

Always wanted to strum a guitar or play the piano? Choose an instrument that neither of you knows and explore it together. Imagine sitting side by side, playing your first duet after weeks of practice—feeling the rhythm, the progress, the joy of finally creating music.

2. Swimming or Skating

Physical activities push us out of our comfort zones. Picture yourself learning to skate with your child—falling, laughing, helping each other up, and finally gliding across the floor with confidence.

3. Pottery or Sculpting

Feel the coolness of clay between your fingers as you shape something from nothing. Pottery is therapeutic, allowing both of you to express creativity through touch. Every uneven, imperfect bowl or figurine will become a treasured reminder of this shared experience.

4. Cooking or Baking

Instead of just feeding your child, why not cook with them? Experiment with new recipes, bake messy cookies, taste failures, and laugh at kitchen disasters. These aren't just cooking lessons—they're memories in the making.

5. Gardening

Start with a tiny balcony garden or a backyard patch. Dig into the soil, plant seeds, and watch life grow together. The patience required for gardening teaches an invaluable lesson: some things take time, and that's okay.

6. Yoga or Meditation

If your child struggles with focus or emotions, yoga can be a beautiful way to center both of you. Picture yourself sitting on mats, breathing deeply, finding stillness together in a world full of distractions.

7. Art and Craft Projects

Unleash creativity through painting, origami, or DIY projects. Let go of perfection—art is about expression, not results. Display your creations at home as a reminder of the time spent together.

8. Photography

Give your child a camera or even a phone, and explore the world through their eyes. Go on mini photography adventures, capturing sunsets, shadows, or the smallest details of everyday life.

9. Fashion Design Basics

Sew simple outfits, design t-shirts, or experiment with colors and patterns. Fashion isn't just about clothing; it's about self-expression and creativity.

The Unexpected Gift of Learning Together

When you learn alongside your child, something remarkable happens:

• You model resilience. They see you struggling, making mistakes, and pushing through—teaching them that learning is never about instant success but about persistence.

• You deepen your bond. Instead of being just their guide, you become their teammate, experiencing joys and setbacks together.

• You rediscover your inner child. The thrill of learning something new reignites the playfulness you thought you had lost.

Now, Close Your Eyes and Imagine

Fast forward a few years.

Your child has grown. Life has moved on. But there's a moment—perhaps in a conversation, a song, or an old photograph—when they recall those days of learning alongside you.

They don't just remember the skill you both learned.

They remember you.

They remember the way you laughed when you both failed, the way you kept going, the way you made learning an adventure rather than a task.

And long after the lessons are over, those memories will remain—etched in their hearts as proof that learning, love, and connection are meant to be lifelong journeys.

Breaking Free: Learning, Earning, and Thriving—Together

Pause for a moment.

Think about your daily routine. The endless cycle of work, responsibility, and survival. You provide for your family, but deep down, something feels missing. The excitement, the passion, the sense of fulfillment—it's faded. You wake up, go to work, return home, and repeat.

And yet, a small voice inside you whispers:

"Is this all there is?"

You're not alone. Many people find themselves stuck in jobs that no longer inspire them, trapped in a routine that drains their enthusiasm. The burden isn't just the work itself—it's the feeling of being stuck, knowing that change is possible but not knowing how to begin.

But here's the truth: It's never too late to rewrite your story.

What if you could reignite your passion while building a more secure future for your family?

What if you could learn new skills alongside your child, turning education into an adventure you both embark on together?

What if, instead of just earning a paycheck, you could create something of lasting value—a life filled with growth, purpose, and freedom?

The journey doesn't require a radical leap. It starts with a simple step.

The Power of Simultaneous Growth

Close your eyes and imagine:

You and your child, side by side, learning something new—not just as an academic exercise, but as a shared experience that could one day transform your lives.

Maybe it's a skill that sparks creativity, like writing, painting, or photography.

Maybe it's something practical, like coding, digital marketing, or woodworking.

Or maybe it's a skill that can eventually create financial independence—a side business, freelancing, or investing.

The skill itself doesn't matter as much as the mindset it builds.

By learning together, you're teaching your child an invaluable lesson:

That life is about constant growth. That it's never too late to start again.
That skills, not circumstances, determine your future.

And most importantly—that they are not alone in their journey.

The 2-Hour Formula for Success

Many people believe they need to dedicate all their time to change their lives. That's why they never start. But the truth is, small, consistent efforts create massive transformation.

Imagine if you and your child committed to just 2 hours a week to learning a skill.

Two hours might seem insignificant. But over the course of a year, that's 104 hours of focused learning. Over two years? 208 hours.

That's the equivalent of a college semester's worth of study—without overwhelming your schedule.

Now, picture this:
• In the first few months, you struggle, experiment, and make mistakes.
• By the end of the first year, you start seeing progress.
• By the second year, the skill is no longer just an experiment—it's something real. Something you can use, something that brings you joy, and maybe even something that earns you money.

Two hours a week. That's all it takes to begin.

Creating Multiple Streams of Income

As you grow in your skill, something amazing happens—you start seeing opportunities you never noticed before.
• A hobby turns into a passion.
• A passion turns into a side gig.
• A side gig turns into an additional stream of income.

Over time, these streams of income add up, creating financial security beyond your primary job. Imagine having the freedom to work on things you love, knowing that you're no longer solely dependent on one paycheck.

And the best part?

Your child is learning alongside you.

They are seeing, firsthand, that income isn't just about finding a job—it's about creating value. They are understanding, through experience, that success isn't about luck but about commitment, persistence, and adaptability.

These lessons are more valuable than anything they'll ever learn in school.

Teaching Your Child the Power of Skill

What if your child grew up without the fear of failure?

What if they saw challenges not as barriers but as opportunities?

When you embark on this journey together, you are teaching them:

• Resilience: That learning something new takes time, effort, and patience.

• Confidence: That they are capable of figuring things out—even when it's hard.

• Adaptability: That no matter where life takes them, they have the skills to thrive.

In a world that's changing faster than ever, these lessons are priceless.

The Bottom Line: A Life Worth Living

The skill you choose doesn't matter as much as the decision to begin.

It's not about quitting your job overnight. It's not about chasing some unrealistic dream.

It's about taking control of your own growth—and inviting your child to grow alongside you.

Imagine looking back five years from now and realizing that these small, weekly efforts completely transformed your life. That you didn't just work to survive—you created a future filled with confidence, purpose, and financial security.

And imagine your child carrying those same lessons forward—into their own career, their own family, their own journey of success.

The best investment you can make isn't in the stock market or real estate.

It's in the skills, mindset, and experiences that shape your future.

Your journey begins now.

Don't wait for the perfect moment. Take the first step today.

Patience

In today's world,

where everything seems to happen at lightning speed, we rarely take a moment to pause and reflect. Whether it's the scrolling through endless content on Instagram or the never-ending autoplay of TikTok videos, these digital distractions have become our norm. But what does this mean for our children?

The rise of short-form video content has profoundly impacted the way children process information. Studies consistently show that increased exposure to platforms like Instagram, TikTok, and YouTube is leading to a decrease in attention span. A study conducted by Common Sense Media in 2019 revealed that 50% of teens admitted that social media distracted them from their schoolwork, while a significant portion of children (around 60%) reported using their phones for several hours daily. The research indicated that the constant exposure to rapidly changing content is rewiring how the brain functions, leading to shorter attention spans and a reduced capacity for patience in real-life situations.

Think about your own life. How often do you feel the urge to check your phone in the middle of a conversation? How many times do you flip through videos or social media posts in search of that instant dopamine hit? Now, imagine this: you've grown up in a world where waiting for anything feels like a lifetime. You were taught to grab what's available right now because that's what feels good. But here's the reality—this habit of instant gratification is shaping how you parent today. Your child mirrors your actions, your urgency, your impatience. You may not see it at first, but it's there.

Case Study: Stanford University (2019)

Stanford University's research on the effect of screen time on patience concluded that children exposed to fast-paced digital environments are less likely to engage in delayed gratification. This was tested through a classic experiment, the Marshmallow Test, where children were offered one marshmallow immediately or two if they waited. Those who spent more time with technology-based entertainment tended to choose immediate rewards over waiting for a greater benefit. The report suggested that the constant "instant gratification" offered by screens made it harder for children to develop patience, leading them to avoid situations that required sustained effort.

Case Study: University of Michigan (2021)

A study by the University of Michigan found a direct correlation between screen time and a decrease in patience. Researchers observed that children who spent more than two hours daily on digital devices exhibited signs of increased irritability and were quicker to express frustration when faced with tasks requiring longer periods of concentration. The study showed that these children had difficulty tolerating any form of waiting, even in low-stakes situations, such as waiting in line or completing a school assignment.

The research linked this frustration tolerance to an inability to solve problems independently. When children are faced with challenging tasks, their first instinct is often to quit or seek an escape, such as resorting to their devices. This avoidance behavior is harmful as it reduces opportunities for critical thinking, patience-building, and problem-solving development.

• Attention Span Decline:

According to a 2018 report by Microsoft, the average human attention span has decreased from 12 seconds in 2000 to just 8 seconds in 2018. The constant bombardment of bite-sized, engaging content on social media is considered a key driver of this change. For children, who are still developing cognitive and emotional skills, this has created a society of instant gratification seekers.

• Problem-Solving Skills:

The American Academy of Pediatrics (2016) highlighted concerns over children's overuse of digital devices, pointing out that less time spent in non-digital play and interaction leads to less development of critical thinking and problem-solving skills. Without the need to "figure things out" or handle delayed gratification, children may struggle with resolving issues independently when faced with obstacles in the real world.

The consequence of this growing impatience is more than just a momentary frustration. Children who regularly indulge in quick-dopamine hits from screen content may experience significant cognitive and emotional delays in managing tasks that require time and patience. The continuous cycle of quick rewards erodes the ability to endure even minor discomforts, leading to a lack of perseverance. The growing trend of instant gratification not only influences how children deal with frustration but also limits their ability to fully engage in creative or academic pursuits that require sustained focus.

These patterns suggest that we must act decisively to counterbalance screen time with activities that foster patience, resilience, and effective problem-solving. This could include encouraging more offline hobbies, games, and exercises that require patience, like puzzles, reading, or even simple outdoor play.

By fostering a balanced environment, we can ensure that children are better equipped to deal with life's challenges, rather than seeking quick and easy escapes through technology.

Consider this:

someone dismisses chess as "boring." On the surface, this may seem like genuine disinterest, but often, it stems from a lack of patience or the absence of someone to guide them through the game's intricacies. Chess, like any meaningful skill, demands effort, persistence, and a willingness to engage with its rules, strategies, and subtleties. Without these, it's easy to mask inexperience or impatience with excuses like, "I don't enjoy it."

This behavior is increasingly common in today's world, especially among children accustomed to the instant gratification provided by screens. These screens, with their rapidly changing visuals and constant stimulation, condition young minds to seek immediate rewards and avoid tasks requiring sustained focus or delayed gratification. This dependency on fleeting entertainment hampers their ability to engage with activities that foster deep learning and skill development.

As parents, educators, or mentors, it's critical to recognize the difference between genuine disinterest and a lack of exposure or effort. Children often need guidance and encouragement to navigate through the initial challenges of a new skill, be it chess or anything else. When left unchecked, the preference for instant gratification may rob them of opportunities to cultivate patience, resilience, and a genuine sense of achievement.

Ask yourself: Is my child's disinterest in learning something new truly theirs, or is it a reflection of an environment overly saturated with easy entertainment? The answer may lead to a deeper understanding of how to nurture their capacity for meaningful growth.

As adults, we understand that real achievement—whether in academics, sports, or the arts—requires persistence, hard work, and the ability to embrace the trial-and-error process.

Success lies in enjoying the journey, not just reaching the destination.

However, the instant dopamine rush children get from screens undermines this understanding. It damages their ability to think critically and sustain the energy required to produce something remarkable.

Fostering Patience and Perseverance in Children

During their formative years, children are easily influenced by their surroundings—be it toys, video games, friends, or gadgets. They often start demanding things simply because others have them. Parents, driven by love or their unmet childhood desires, sometimes fulfil these demands without questioning their necessity. While this might provide short-term happiness, it deprives the child of learning an essential life lesson: patience.

Life does not always give us what we want immediately. Often, we must work hard and wait for results. Teaching children to wait for what they desire helps them appreciate the value of effort and understand the difference between genuine needs and impulsive wants. Fulfilling every demand instantly might make parents feel proud, but it can leave children ill-equipped to face life's challenges, which often test our patience and perseverance.

In the late 1960s, psychologist Walter Mischel conducted an experiment that would later become one of the most famous studies in understanding self-control and its long-term impact. The study involved preschool-aged children, each placed alone in a room with a single marshmallow on the table. They were given a choice: they could eat the marshmallow immediately or wait for the researcher to return after a short absence, typically about 15 minutes, and be rewarded with a second marshmallow. This simple scenario tested the child's ability to delay gratification in favor of a greater reward.

What made this study so impactful were its long-term findings. Decades later, researchers followed up with the children, now adults, and found a striking pattern. Those who had resisted the immediate temptation tended to have better outcomes in various aspects of life, including academic achievement, stress management, and even relationships. The ability to delay gratification, as demonstrated in this experiment, appeared to correlate with a higher likelihood of success and stability in life.

This experiment teaches a powerful lesson for parents today. Self-control and patience are not innate traits but skills that can be nurtured, especially in a world dominated by instant rewards and digital distractions. However, it's equally important to recognize that factors like a child's environment and sense of security also play significant roles in shaping their behavior. The marshmallow test reminds us that fostering patience in children requires not just guidance but also creating an atmosphere of trust and consistency—elements that are often overshadowed in the fast-paced, screen-heavy lives we lead today.

Children need to learn that the world is filled with distractions designed to provoke impulsive decisions. Success, however, is the result of sustained efforts and thoughtful actions. Reprogramming an impulsive mind to one that values patience and perseverance can unlock a child's full potential.

Parents can instil these traits in their children through meaningful lessons and everyday practices.

For instance, when a child demands something, evaluate the real purpose behind the request. Encourage them to work or wait for it, making the reward more meaningful.

The Magic Plant

One sunny morning, Kiara ran up to me, her eyes sparkling with excitement. "Papa, can I have a big, beautiful flower plant in my room? Like the one we saw at the nursery yesterday!"

I smiled at her enthusiasm. "Of course, Kiara. But how about we grow one ourselves instead of buying it?"

She tilted her head. "Grow one? But that will take so long! Can't we just buy it?"

I sat down beside her and said, "Sometimes, the things we wait for and work towards are more special than the ones we get instantly. If we grow a plant together, it will teach us patience and care. What do you say?"

She hesitated for a moment but then nodded. "Okay, Papa. Let's grow one!"

The Journey Begins

We went to the nursery that evening and picked out a packet of sunflower seeds. Back home, I showed her how to prepare a pot with soil and plant the seeds. Kiara carefully placed each seed in the soil, her tiny fingers working with precision.

"Now what, Papa?" she asked eagerly.

"Now," I said, "we water it a little and wait. Every day, we'll take care of it, but it will take time before we see the first sprout."

Her face fell slightly. "How long?"

"About a week for the sprout, and a few months for the flower," I said, ruffling her hair.

"A few months?" she gasped. "That's forever!"

I laughed. "It feels that way, but patience is like a superpower, Kiara. When we wait and take care of something, it becomes even more beautiful. You'll see."

Learning Patience

The first few days were exciting for her. Kiara eagerly watered the pot every morning and checked it throughout the day. "Is it growing yet, Papa?" she would ask.

"Not yet, Kiara," I said. "But it's working hard underground. Just like you need time to grow taller, the seed needs time to grow, too."

By the fourth day, her excitement began to wane. "This is taking too long," she complained.

"Good things take time," I reminded her. "How about we make a deal? Every time we check the plant, we'll also do something fun together—like draw or play a game. That way, the waiting won't feel so hard."

She agreed, and soon our routine became something more. We'd water the plant and then spend time together reading stories, painting pictures, or just talking about our day. The waiting started to feel less like waiting and more like bonding.

The First Sprout

On the seventh day, Kiara ran into the kitchen, shouting, "Papa! Papa! Come quickly!"

I followed her to the pot, and there it was—a tiny green sprout poking through the soil. Her face lit up with pure joy. "It's growing, Papa! It's really growing!"

I knelt beside her. "See what patience can do? If we had bought a flower, we wouldn't have felt this happy. But because you waited and cared for it, this little sprout feels so special."

She nodded, her smile wide. "It's like a magic plant!"

The Transformation

Over the next few months, Kiara's excitement never wavered. She watered the plant every day, adjusted its position to get sunlight, and even talked to it. When the first sunflower finally bloomed, she couldn't contain her pride.

"Look, Papa!" she said, holding the pot. "We did it!"

"Yes, we did," I said. "And do you know what made this flower so beautiful?"

"What?" she asked.

"Your patience," I said. "You waited, you cared, and you didn't give up. That's what made this flower so special. And that's the same magic you can use in life—whether it's learning something new or reaching a big goal. Good things take time, Kiara, but they're always worth the wait."

She hugged me tightly, her little hands around my neck. "Thank you, Papa. I'll always remember this."

Reflection

That sunflower stayed in Kiara's room for months, a constant reminder of the value of patience and care. And every time she faced a challenge or felt impatient, I'd point to the sunflower and say, "Remember, Kiara—good things take time."

CHAPTER TWELVE

The Comparison Trap

The Silent Thief of Childhood: How Jealousy and Envy Take Root

Imagine planting a garden, carefully selecting the best seeds for vibrant flowers and nourishing fruits. But one day, a small weed appears. At first, it seems harmless—barely noticeable. Yet, as time passes, it spreads, choking the life out of the plants you nurtured. This is how jealousy and envy grow in a child's mind—silently, subtly, and dangerously.

What starts as a passing comparison can turn into a lifelong habit of self-doubt, resentment, and missed potential. A child who constantly measures themselves against others loses sight of their own strengths, draining their energy and confidence. Instead of focusing on personal growth, they become stuck in a cycle of inferiority and frustration.

But it doesn't have to be this way. As parents, we have the power to reshape this narrative—to pull the weeds before they overtake the garden. By shifting our words, fostering gratitude, and encouraging self-improvement over comparison, we can help children break free from jealousy's grip and embrace their own unique journey.

The Adverse Effects of Jealousy and Envy on a Child's Growth

Imagine your mind as a car engine. When fueled by positivity, ambition, and gratitude, it roars to life, charging ahead toward your potential. But jealousy is like a clog in the engine. It's a constant drag on your power.

1. Energy Drain: Jealousy consumes energy. Instead of focusing on what you're good at, you're fixated on someone else's success. It's like trying to

run a race with a backpack full of rocks—every step feels heavier. Rahul spends more time stewing over Arya's popularity than honing his own talents.

2. Damaged Self-Worth: Envy can create an internal narrative of inadequacy. You think, "Why am I not as good as them?" rather than, "How can I become better?" This leaves children feeling worthless and disconnected from their true potential.

3. Lack of Teamwork: A child who's consumed by jealousy can't be a good team member. They're always measuring themselves against others, rather than collaborating and building. In group work, they're the one thinking, "Why should I help them? I should be the one leading." This can cause isolation and missed opportunities for learning.

4. A Fixed Mindset: When kids believe that abilities are fixed—either you're born good at something or you're not—they focus more on avoiding failure than on learning. Jealousy reinforces this mindset, making them think that success is a zero-sum game, and if someone else wins, it means they've lost.

A Lesson in the Playground

One evening, Kiara came home from the park with her arms crossed and a storm brewing in her little eyes.

"I don't want to play with Manya anymore," she blurted out, throwing her shoes aside.

I looked up from my book. "Why? What happened?"

"She always wins the running race. Always! No matter how fast I run, she's faster." Kiara's voice cracked between frustration and disappointment. "It's not fair!"

I closed my book and pulled her onto my lap. "So, you're upset because she's better at running?"

She nodded, her lips pursed.

I smiled and pointed at the bookshelf. "Do you see all those stories? Some are about heroes, some about scientists, some about artists. Every story is different, just like every person. If you only focus on the parts where others shine, you'll forget about the chapters where you're the hero."

She listened, but her brows remained furrowed.

I continued, "Let me ask you something—what do you love doing the most?"

"Drawing," she answered immediately.

"Right! And does Manya draw as well as you?"

Kiara thought for a moment, then shook her head. "No... she doesn't like drawing much."

I nodded. "Exactly. Imagine if Manya got upset every time you drew something beautiful. Would that make sense?"

A small smile crept onto her face.

"So instead of feeling bad about Manya's running, why not learn from her? Ask her how she runs so fast, practice with her, and see if you can improve. Compete with yourself, not with her."

She was quiet for a moment, then her shoulders relaxed. "Maybe I can ask her to teach me."

I ruffled her hair. "That's my girl."

That night, as she drifted off to sleep, she whispered, "I think tomorrow I'll race Manya again... but this time, just to see if I can beat my time."

I smiled in the darkness. The first weed had been pulled before it could take root.

The Power of Perspective

Children, like gardens, grow in the direction they are nurtured. If left unchecked, jealousy and envy can tangle around their confidence, stunting their growth. But with the right guidance, we can shift their perspective—from comparison to self-improvement, from resentment to admiration, from insecurity to self-belief.

The question is—how do we, as parents, make sure we're planting the right seeds before it's too late?

The Road to Growth: How Parents Can Shift the Mindset

Now that we've seen how jealousy can impede a child's progress, let's discuss how to turn things around. Here's how parents can help their kids develop a growth mindset—one where they embrace challenges, learn from mistakes, and thrive in their own unique abilities.

1. Shift the Focus from "Better Than" to "Better At"

Instead of telling your child to be more like someone else, emphasize the unique qualities that make them great. Instead of saying, "Why can't you be more like Arya?" try saying, "What's one thing you admire about Arya? How can you bring that kind of energy to what you do?"

Example: Let's say your child is struggling with math while a friend excels. Instead of letting jealousy take root, you can say, "I admire how your friend practices math regularly. What steps can you take to practice and get better? You have your own way of approaching challenges." This helps the child focus on self-improvement rather than comparison.

2. Praise Effort Over Outcome

The trick is to praise the process, not just the end result. When kids feel like they're only valued for their success, they start measuring themselves solely by how they stack up against others. Instead, celebrate the effort they put into something, even if the result isn't perfect.

Example: If your child creates a drawing but it's not exactly like the one they saw online, praise their creativity. "I love how you added your own twist to it! You worked so hard on this, and that's what really matters." This reinforces the idea that growth comes from the journey, not just the destination.

3. Encourage Healthy Competition

Competition isn't bad in itself—it's the way it's approached that matters. Teach your child to compete with themselves rather than others. "Can you beat your own score?" is a healthier question than, "Can you beat everyone else?"

Example: If your child is learning to ride a bike, don't compare them to the neighbor's kid who's already an expert. Encourage them to set small goals for themselves, like riding a little further every day. This empowers them to measure success by their own growth.

4. Teach Gratitude and Self-Awareness

Gratitude helps children see the value in what they have and who they are, reducing the urge to compare. You can help your child by regularly asking them, "What are three things you're thankful for today?" This helps them appreciate their own strengths and what makes them unique.

Example: After a playdate, sit down with your child and ask, "What did you enjoy most about today? What was something new you learned?" This helps your child focus on their own experiences rather than looking at what others have.

5. Normalize Imperfection and Failure

Show your child that it's okay to fail and that failure is just a stepping stone to success. When they see mistakes as part of the learning process, they'll be less likely to feel inferior when others succeed.

Example: Share stories of your own failures. "I didn't get that promotion because I didn't prepare well. But I learned from it, and next time, I'll be ready!" This teaches them that growth comes from learning—not from being perfect.

6. Role-Play Positive Self-Talk

Children often internalize their parents' words. Teach your child to counter jealousy with positive affirmations and self-talk.

Example: If your child feels jealous of a friend's success, help them reframe the situation. "Instead of feeling upset, let's think about what we can learn from them. What's something you admire about them that you can apply to your own life?"

7. Lead by Example

Children are great mimics. When they see their parents dealing with jealousy or failure in a healthy way, they learn how to do the same. If you feel envious of someone, talk about it openly but show how you handle it.

Example: If a colleague gets recognition for a project, you might say, "I admire the work they did, and it inspires me to work harder. I'll learn from their approach." This helps your child see that it's okay to admire others and use that energy to grow themselves.

8. Be Their Biggest Cheerleader—Without Overindulgence

Cheer on your child's efforts, but without inflating their sense of entitlement. Help them realize that praise should be earned, and that their self-worth doesn't come from external validation.

Example: If your child receives praise for a school project, instead of saying, "You're the best in the class!" say, "I'm really proud of how hard you worked on this. Your effort shows in your work." This reinforces the value of effort, not just outcome.

Final Thought: Nurturing a Growth Mindset Is Like Tending to a Garden

As a parent, you're the gardener. You have the power to prune the weeds of jealousy and envy, water the seeds of effort and self-belief, and watch your child grow into a strong, independent, and confident individual. The journey won't always be easy, but with patience, consistency, and care, you can help your child build a mindset that focuses on growth, not comparison.

CHAPTER THIRTEEN

The Dispute

Parents, we need to talk. Not about your child's screen time, grades, or eating habits, but about something more profound: the relationship between you and your partner. You might think your conflicts are private matters, but in reality, they have front-row seats in your child's mind, shaping their worldview and future relationships.

Every disagreement—be it over household chores or financial decisions—leaves an imprint. When these disputes become loud or prolonged, they introduce tension into your child's environment, affecting their sense of security. Research indicates that high levels of conflict between parents place children at a greater risk of developing emotional, social, and behavioral problems.

Children are not just passive observers; they internalize the dynamics they witness. Studies show that parental conflict can lead to increased risks of depression, anxiety, and lowered self-esteem in children. Over time, these experiences can distort their understanding of relationships, making them believe that conflict is an inherent aspect of love.

Reflect on your disputes. How often do they escalate over trivial matters, fueled by ego rather than genuine issues? Such conflicts not only strain your relationship but also serve as negative examples for your child, teaching them unhealthy ways to handle disagreements.

The implications extend beyond the immediate family. The environment you create at home serves as a blueprint for your child's future interactions. A nurturing and respectful atmosphere fosters positive mental well-being, while a contentious one can lead to adverse outcomes.

Consider this: children who observe respectful communication and conflict resolution are more likely to emulate these behaviors in their own relationships. Conversely, exposure to constant discord can result in fear, anger, anxiety, and sadness, increasing the risk of various health problems.

It's easy to dismiss these concerns as exaggerated. However, numerous studies have traced issues like trust deficits, low self-esteem, and destructive behaviors back to unresolved childhood experiences stemming from parental conflict. These early exposures don't remain dormant; they manifest in adulthood, affecting one's ability to form healthy relationships and cope with challenges.

Reflect on your own upbringing. How did your parents' relationship influence your perceptions and mental health? By acknowledging and addressing the impact of your behavior, you can break the cycle of generational trauma and foster a healthier environment for your child.

In conclusion, it's imperative to recognize that your interactions with your partner profoundly affect your child's development. By fostering a harmonious and respectful relationship, you not only strengthen your bond but also provide your child with a solid foundation for their mental and emotional well-being.

The Echoes of Our Words: A Lesson in Love and Resolution

It started with something small—something that, in the moment, felt trivial. A misplaced water bottle, a missed errand, an offhand comment said in exhaustion. My wife and I had been bickering more than usual, the stress of daily life weighing on us. Work, responsibilities, and the constant juggle of parenting left us with little patience for each other. Our words grew sharper, our silences longer.

At first, we thought the children didn't notice. Kiara, our elder daughter, was her usual curious self, asking endless questions about the world, while Kyna, just a baby, was too young to understand. Or so we believed.

Then, one evening, everything changed.

We were in the middle of another disagreement—this time over something as mundane as forgotten groceries. Frustration built up quickly, and our voices, though not screaming, carried the unmistakable weight of irritation. Midway through our argument, Kiara, who had been playing nearby, suddenly dropped her crayons.

She didn't say anything, but I noticed her hands clutching her dress tightly. Her usual bright eyes darted between us, her small shoulders tense.

"Kiara, what happened?" I asked, my voice instantly softening.

She hesitated before whispering, "Are you and Mama angry... like really angry?"

Her words hit me harder than I expected.

I glanced at my wife, and I could see the same realization washing over her. Kiara's little face was lined with worry—a worry no four-year-old should carry. I knelt beside her and pulled her into my arms.

"No, sweetheart," I said gently. "Mama and I are just... talking a little loud."

She didn't look convinced. "But you both sound like you don't like each other. Did I do something wrong?"

My heart sank. How many times had I assumed she wasn't paying attention? How many times had she picked up on the tension we thought we were hiding?

That night, after putting the girls to sleep, my wife and I sat down for a long conversation.

"We need to change," she said, her voice filled with regret. "I never want them to think our love for them—or for each other—is fragile."

I nodded. "They're not just hearing our words. They're feeling our emotions. We're teaching them how relationships work, whether we realize it or not."

And so, we made a silent promise.

It wasn't about never disagreeing. Conflicts were inevitable. But we would learn to resolve them differently. No raised voices near the children. No cold silences that made the house feel heavier. If we had to argue, we'd do it behind closed doors, after calming down. More importantly, we'd work on listening—really listening—to each other.

Over the next few weeks, the change was subtle but powerful.

Kiara, who had been growing quieter during our tense days, started opening up again, her laughter returning in full force. Kyna, too young to speak, responded to the shift with more smiles, her little giggles filling the house.

One day, as I helped Kiara with her drawings, she looked up at me and said, "Papa, you and Mama don't talk loud anymore. I like it this way."

I hugged her tightly, realizing that in trying to be better parents, we had also become better partners.

Our children had been the mirror we needed—to show us how much our words, our tone, and even our silences shaped their world.

And in that realization, we found not just a resolution, but a renewed love for each other and the family we were building.

So, what can you do? Let's get practical (and maybe a little funny):

1. Hit Pause on the Drama.

Seriously, imagine a big, invisible "Pause" button floating in front of you during an argument. Use it. If you feel like yelling, stop, breathe, and grab a glass of water instead. Bonus points if you can drink it dramatically and say, "I'm hydrating instead of fighting."

2. Communicate Like Grown-Ups.

I know it's tempting to score points in an argument, but remember, this isn't a game. Sit down with your partner when you're both calm, and talk like adults. No shouting, no sarcasm, no bringing up that one thing from five years ago. Focus on listening, not just replying.

3. Let the Kids See the Good Stuff.

It's okay for your child to know that conflicts happen—life isn't always sunshine and unicorns. But let them see how you resolve those conflicts. Apologize when you're wrong (yes, even if it hurts your ego), and make up in front of them. Show them that love is about forgiveness and teamwork, not just winning.

4. Teach Emotional Intelligence.

Talk to your kids about emotions. Use simple examples: "You know how you feel frustrated when your Lego tower falls? That's how Mommy and Daddy feel sometimes too. But instead of getting angry, we're learning to fix the tower together."

5. Laugh a Little.

Honestly, a little humor can defuse even the tensest situations. The next time you're in the middle of an argument about something silly, stop and laugh at how ridiculous it is. "We're really arguing about socks on the floor? Let's just donate all our socks and be barefoot forever!"

6. Seek Help if Needed.

If the arguments feel too big to handle, don't hesitate to ask for professional help. Therapy isn't a sign of failure—it's a tool for growth.

At the end of the day, remember this: your child doesn't need perfect parents. They need parents who are willing to grow, adapt, and show them that love is stronger than any argument. Create a home where respect, kindness, and laughter reign. You're not just shaping your child's future—you're shaping the world they'll live in.

So, let's take a step back, breathe, and choose love over ego.

Because in the end,

The best gift you can give your child isn't a fancy gadget or a lavish birthday party—it's the security of knowing that, no matter what, their parents are a team.

CHAPTER FOURTEEN

The Role of Food

As parents, it's vital to recognize the profound connection between the food we consume and the health, mindset, and overall well-being we cultivate. What we eat isn't just sustenance—it becomes part of us, shaping every cell in our bodies. This deep understanding of food is a legacy that you have the opportunity to pass on to your child, embedding the values of mindful eating and health-conscious choices into the next generation.

Take a moment to reflect on how you approach food: the ingredients you choose, the meals you prepare, and the way you fuel your body. Much of this wisdom may have come from your parents or the lessons you've gathered over the years. Now, it's time to share this with your child. Early childhood is a crucial window for this learning because children, at this age, are naturally curious and eager to absorb information. As they grow older, particularly during the teenage years, they may become more resistant to your guidance. That's why it's essential to plant these seeds of knowledge early, while their minds are open and receptive.

Many families, I've noticed, have developed a routine where meals are often consumed in isolation or, if they sit together, each individual is engrossed in their own screen—whether it's a phone, tablet, or the common distraction of a TV show playing in the background. While this is a norm in many homes, it's important to recognize that mealtime holds incredible potential beyond just nourishment. Eating is one of the most vital moments of the day, where our bodies absorb essential nutrients that fuel us, helping us grow and become better versions of ourselves. Yet, in many households, this time is often spent distracted, leaving little room for meaningful connection.

I began to realize that this time could be so much more—it could be an opportunity for life-changing conversations, bonding, and learning. Sitting down for a meal with your child isn't just about food; it's an invitation to open up and connect. Rather than letting screens take away from this experience, I began to think of mealtime as a chance to engage in a deeper dialogue with my children and family.

When we sit together to eat, I try to weave in meaningful conversations about our family's food traditions. I share the stories behind certain dishes—why we prepare them, how we've chosen specific ingredients, and how certain meals became staples in our household. I explain how food plays a central role in our health and well-being, speaking in a way that is simple and relatable. For instance, I tell my children how eating vegetables like spinach or carrots helps strengthen their body, or how fruits like oranges boost their immunity and give them energy to play and learn.

These conversations aren't just about educating them; they're about instilling an appreciation for the food we eat and the effort that goes into preparing it. This shared time not only builds their understanding of the food's nutritional value but also teaches them the importance of mindful eating and appreciating the effort that goes into making a meal. The act of talking and bonding over food helps create memories that go beyond just the physical nourishment; it fosters a connection that strengthens the family unit.

Turning mealtime into a moment of connection, learning, and appreciation has not only enriched our family dynamic but has also allowed us to grow together. It's a simple yet profound shift in how we spend our time, and it has become one of the most cherished parts of our day.

In today's fast-paced world, the allure of junk food is ever-present, with its convenience and marketing targeting young, impressionable minds. If children don't develop an understanding of food early on, they're more likely to be swayed by unhealthy eating habits. Fast food and processed snacks can harm not just their physical health—leading to weakened immune systems—but also their mental clarity and emotional balance. In contrast, home-cooked meals, prepared with love and care, carry energy and nourishment that go beyond just calories. They represent connection, tradition, and well-being.

To counteract the pervasive influence of unhealthy food culture, make meal times an opportunity for gentle, engaging discussions. Talk about why certain foods are good for your family's health, how they've been part of your diet for generations, and their significance for your body type and lifestyle. For example, you could explain why soups are great during winter, how certain fruits are ideal for hot summers, or the science behind including leafy greens in your meals. By framing these conversations scientifically and meaningfully, your child will see food as not just something to eat but as an essential part of living well.

Moreover, these lessons in mindful eating will cultivate self-reliance and confidence in your child. When children understand why they eat what they eat, they're better equipped to make informed choices, even when faced with societal pressures to conform to unhealthy habits. This knowledge becomes a shield, protecting their self-esteem and encouraging them to prioritize their well-being over fleeting indulgences.

Ultimately, the role of food in your family is about more than health—it's about fostering a mindset of mindfulness, appreciation, and self-care. Every meal is an opportunity to connect, educate, and create a legacy that will empower your child to navigate the complexities of the world with a strong body, a clear mind, and a resilient spirit.

10-Step Strategy for Transforming Mealtime into a Life-Changing Experience

This strategy is designed to be actionable, easy to adopt from day one, and highly effective in creating a lifelong positive impact on your child's eating habits, mindset, and overall well-being.

Step 1: Make Family Meals a Priority

• Commit to at least one meal a day where everyone sits together without screens.

• Start small—even if it's just breakfast or dinner, consistency is key.

Step 2: Remove All Distractions (No Screens at the Table)

• Create a strict no-phone, no-TV rule during meals to encourage mindful eating.

• Use this time for family conversations, storytelling, or discussing the day.

Step 3: Educate Through Stories and Simple Science

• Instead of forcing healthy food, tell engaging stories about its benefits.

• Example: "Spinach makes you strong like superheroes because it has iron!"

• Share how food affects mood, energy, and growth in a fun way.

Step 4: Involve Children in Meal Preparation

• Let them wash vegetables, mix ingredients, or set the table based on their age.

• This makes them excited about food and more likely to eat what they helped prepare.

Step 5: Create a Weekly Food Tradition

• Example: "Healthy Sunday Brunch" or "Friday Family Cooking"

• Cook a new nutritious meal together each week and explore different food traditions.

Step 6: Make Healthy Eating a Choice, Not a Rule

• Offer two healthy options instead of saying, "Eat this."

• Example: "Would you like carrot sticks or cucumber slices with your meal?"

• This empowers children and builds self-reliance in food choices.

Step 7: Teach Seasonal and Cultural Food Awareness

• Talk about why certain foods are best for different seasons and body needs.

• Example: "Mangoes give energy in summer, while soups keep us warm in winter."

Step 8: Slowly Reduce Processed and Junk Food

• Instead of banning junk food, replace it gradually with homemade alternatives.

• Example: Swap packaged chips for homemade baked potato wedges or nuts.

Step 9: Celebrate Small Wins and Appreciate Effort

• Praise children for trying new foods or helping in the kitchen.

• Example: "I love how you helped mix the salad! That made it extra delicious."

Step 10: Lead by Example

• Children follow what they see. If you eat mindfully and enjoy healthy meals, they will too.

• Show enthusiasm when eating fruits, vegetables, and home-cooked food.

By consistently applying this strategy, you'll create a home environment where food is more than just nutrition—it becomes a source of connection, learning, and lifelong healthy habits.

CHAPTER FIFTEEN

The Perfect Bedtime Routine

The bedtime routine is one of the most precious opportunities for a parent to bond deeply with their child.

Typically, parents guide their children through steps like brushing their teeth, moisturizing their skin, putting on cosy nightwear, and ensuring they are warm and comfortable, protected from the weather. On the surface, this routine seems perfect—it takes care of a child's physical well-being.

However, bedtime holds immense potential for nurturing a child's mental growth, thought processes, emotional intelligence, and inner strength. This can be achieved by creating a magical world filled with fictional characters that revolve around your child.

Imagine crafting a story where the central character mirrors certain traits of your child. Give this character a name that resonates with them, something they can easily visualize and relate to. Develop a story where the character faces challenges, seeks help, and transforms into a stronger, more emotionally intelligent version of themselves. The story should be filled with humour, engaging moments, and a clear moral value.

As you narrate, paint a vivid picture. Describe the setting—its colours, light, sounds, and surroundings—so richly that it feels real to your child. Let the moral of the story flow naturally into their hearts, creating a mesmerizing effect that lingers as they drift into sleep. This storytelling not only entertains but leaves a lasting imprint on their subconscious mind, programming it with positive values and lessons.

"But I'm not a storyteller!"

You might wonder, "How can I develop such stories when I'm not a skilled storyteller?" Or, "The ready-made storybooks I've tried don't seem to engage my child the way I'd hoped."

Here's the solution: Technology.

1. Create a Character: Think of a character name that your child will love.

2. Use an AI Tool: Use ChatGPT, Google Gemini, or any other AI tool on your device. Provide specific instructions like:

• The desired story length (e.g., 10 minutes).

• The name of the hero/heroine.

• The setting (e.g., jungle, bedroom, playground).

• The moral or lesson you want to convey.

• A challenge the character faces and the transformation they undergo.

The AI tool will generate a personalized story tailored to your child's needs. Every day, you can create a new story with fresh ideas and morals.

As you narrate the story, pause occasionally to involve your child. Ask them what they think will happen next, and adapt the story based on their imagination. This interaction will make the experience even more immersive and meaningful.

Example: Teaching the Importance of Brushing Teeth

Suppose you want to instil the habit of regular brushing. You could ask your AI tool for a story like this:

"Create a 15-minute story for a 7-year-old. The main character, Alex, skips brushing their teeth out of laziness, develops a toothache and learns a lesson after a visit to the dentist. Include a vivid narrative about mischievous 'tooth monsters' and highlight the importance of brushing regularly."

Here's an example story you might receive:

Alex and the Mischievous Tooth Monsters

Seven-year-old Alex had a habit. Every night before bed, when Mom or Dad said, "Don't forget to brush your teeth!" Alex would reply, "I will!" but sneakily skip it. "It takes too long," Alex would mutter. "And nothing bad ever happens!"

One morning, Alex woke up with a strange, dull ache in their mouth. "Ouch," Alex groaned, touching their cheek. Breakfast didn't help, especially when a bite of cold cereal made the pain worse.

"Alex, what's wrong?" Mom asked.

"My tooth hurts," Alex confessed, wincing.

Mom sighed knowingly. "I think it's time we visit Dr. Smiles, the dentist. Let's go today."

Alex didn't like the sound of that but nodded reluctantly.

The Truth About Tooth Monsters

Dr. Smiles was a cheerful man with a kind face. When Alex sat nervously in the dentist's chair, he turned on a little flashlight and said, "Let's see what's going on here."

As Dr. Smiles examined Alex's teeth, he chuckled. "Ah, I see what's happening. The Tooth Monsters have been busy in here!"

Alex sat up, surprised. "Tooth Monsters?"

Dr. Smiles nodded with a serious expression. "Oh, yes. You see, Tooth Monsters LOVE when we don't brush our teeth. They're tiny little creatures that hide between your teeth. They munch on leftover food bits and grow stronger. If you don't brush them away, they throw wild parties and leave behind 'cavity caves.' That's what's causing your toothache."

Alex's eyes widened. "Really? There are monsters in my teeth?"

"Let me show you," Dr. Smiles said. He picked up a little mirror and pointed to a small black spot on one of Alex's teeth. "See that? That's where the Tooth Monsters built their cave."

The Tooth Monsters' Mischief

That night, as Alex lay in bed, they couldn't stop imagining the mischievous Tooth Monsters. In their mind, the monsters were tiny, with jellybean-shaped bodies and wobbly legs. They giggled and cheered every time Alex skipped brushing.

"Party time!" one monster shouted. "No toothbrush tonight!"

Another added, "Quick, find all the food crumbs from lunch and dinner. Let's build more caves!"

They danced around, leaving sticky, sugary footprints all over Alex's teeth.

Learning the Lesson

The next morning, Alex looked in the bathroom mirror, imagining the Tooth Monsters laughing and celebrating. "Not this time," Alex said with determination.

They picked up their toothbrush and started scrubbing. "Take that, you Tooth Monsters!" Alex said aloud, brushing every corner of their mouth.

For the next few days, Alex brushed morning and night. After their follow-up visit with Dr. Smiles, the dentist smiled proudly. "Great work, Alex! The Tooth Monsters are packing their bags. No more parties in here!"

Alex grinned. "They're not coming back. Ever."

From that day on, brushing became a part of Alex's daily routine. And every night, as Alex brushed, they imagined the Tooth Monsters running away, shaking their tiny fists and grumbling, "Nooooo, not the toothbrush!"

The Takeaway

The story of the Tooth Monsters stuck with Alex forever. They realized that skipping brushing wasn't just laziness—it was an invitation for mischief and pain. And now, Alex brushed every day, knowing they were the hero of their teeth, keeping the Tooth Monsters far, far away.

This 15-minute story uses a vivid narrative with relatable characters to highlight the importance of brushing teeth and the consequences of neglecting it. Let me know if you'd like any adjustments!

Through such stories, your child not only learns practical habits but also connects with you on a deeper level. They experience bedtime as a magical adventure, full of lessons and love, strengthening their bond while shaping their values.

By creating personalized stories infused with moral lessons, cultural values, etiquette, and deep emotional connections, you transform bedtime into a magical and enriching experience for your child. This routine not only strengthens the bond between you and your child but also gradually instils life lessons and values memorably and engagingly. The personalized story world you craft becomes a powerful tool for nurturing your child's character while making bedtime a cherished and meaningful part of their day.

Children perceive stories in a unique, imaginative, and deeply personal way. Unlike adults, who analyze stories through logic and context, children dive into them emotionally and visually. They don't just hear a story—they live it. As a story unfolds, a child's mind creates vivid images of the characters, settings, and events. They imagine the hero's bravery, the villain's menace, and the challenges being overcome as if they were part of the journey. This immersive engagement allows children to connect with the emotions and lessons embedded in the narrative. Through stories, they grasp complex concepts—like honesty, kindness, or courage—more naturally than through direct instruction, as they can relate to characters and see the consequences of choices unfold.

Cultures around the world have long recognized the power of storytelling to impart values and life lessons. From folktales passed down by elders to myths about gods and heroes, stories encapsulate the essence of a culture's wisdom. They serve as a bridge between generations, carrying forward morals, traditions, and shared identity. For children, stories aren't just entertainment—they're a tool for understanding the world. A tale about a clever fox might teach resourcefulness, while a story about a kind king might emphasize the value of compassion. These narratives resonate deeply because they simplify life's complexities into relatable situations that a child can grasp and emulate.

When children imagine a story, their minds weave together the narrative, filling in gaps with their own creativity. A tale of a magical forest might inspire them to picture their favorite park transformed into an enchanted land. They assign traits to characters, imagining their expressions, voices, and movements. This creative process not only nurtures their imagination but also helps them internalize the story's moral. A story about a selfless act of kindness, for example, doesn't just teach them to be kind—it shows them how kindness feels, looks, and impacts others. This emotional engagement cements the lesson in their hearts and minds.

A well-told story with strong moral values and compelling characters becomes a guide for children, teaching them to navigate life's challenges. By witnessing the struggles and triumphs of fictional heroes, children learn empathy, resilience, and the impact of their actions. Unlike lectures or instructions, which can feel abstract or distant, stories touch their emotions and leave lasting impressions. They inspire children to reflect on their choices and emulate the virtues they admire in the characters.

Ultimately, storytelling is a timeless tool for nurturing a child's moral compass. A good story not only entertains but also plants seeds of wisdom, helping children grow into thoughtful, empathetic individuals. By infusing your stories with strong morals, engaging characters, and relatable scenarios, you're doing more than sharing a tale—you're shaping the foundation of a child's character and values, giving them a roadmap for a meaningful life.

Bedtime stories are far more than a comforting ritual; they play a crucial role in shaping a child's emotional, cognitive, and psychological development. As a child listens to a story before sleep, their brain shifts into slower, more receptive states like alpha and theta, allowing the story's lessons and emotions to deeply influence the subconscious mind. This makes bedtime stories a powerful tool for subtly instilling values, such as courage, kindness, and resilience, in a way that feels natural and memorable. The calming rhythm of storytelling also helps a child relax, signaling the transition to sleep and fostering the release of melatonin, which improves sleep quality. Imaginative tales ignite creativity and empathy, as children visualize new worlds and relate to the emotions of the characters, shaping their emotional intelligence. Furthermore, the act of storytelling strengthens the parent-child bond, creating a sense of trust, security, and love that lingers long after the story ends. Over time, the morals and lessons embedded in these narratives become part of the child's internal compass, influencing how they perceive and interact with the world. A bedtime story is not just a moment of connection; it is a lifelong gift, nurturing a child's imagination, values, and sense of self.

Here is a reference material you must follow when you feel limited with your ideas.

The Panchatantra and Hitopadesha are among the most celebrated collections of fables in Indian literature, revered for their timeless wisdom and universal appeal. These ancient texts, though written centuries ago, continue to inspire readers across the globe, transcending cultural and linguistic boundaries. Both collections are rooted in the rich tradition of storytelling in India, blending morality, practical wisdom, and imaginative narratives in ways that captivate and enlighten readers of all ages.

The Panchatantra, often referred to as a treasure trove of animal fables, is believed to have been composed by Vishnu Sharma around 200 BCE, though the exact date of its origin remains debated. Legend has it that Vishnu Sharma, a wise scholar, was tasked with teaching three unruly princes the art of governance and practical wisdom. To make learning engaging, he wove life lessons into a series of stories featuring animals as protagonists. Each tale was crafted to convey profound truths about human behavior, relationships, and leadership. Divided into five books, or "tantras," the Panchatantra addresses themes such as friendship, conflict resolution, strategy, and the consequences of actions, making it a manual for practical living.

The Hitopadesha ("Beneficial Advice") draws heavily from the Panchatantra but presents its teachings in a more concise and poetic form. Authored by Narayana, likely around the 9th or 10th century CE, this text was designed to impart moral and political guidance in a way that resonated with a broader audience. Like its predecessor, the Hitopadesha uses animals to personify human traits, making complex ideas relatable and easy to grasp. Its stories often revolve around themes of loyalty, cunning, greed, and the importance of making wise choices.

Both the Panchatantra and Hitopadesha encapsulate India's cultural heritage, reflecting its philosophical depth and moral values. These stories are not mere entertainment; they serve as mirrors to human society, offering insights into virtues, flaws, and the interplay of destiny and effort. They encapsulate the oral storytelling tradition of ancient India, where lessons were passed down through engaging narratives rather than didactic lectures. The use of animals as characters makes the stories universally relatable, transcending barriers of time, geography, and culture.

What makes these fables particularly powerful is their ability to ignite the imagination. By placing human dilemmas in the context of animal interactions, the stories encourage readers to think creatively and empathetically. A child imagining a clever fox or a loyal elephant engages in a form of cognitive play, learning to see the world from different perspectives. This imaginative engagement fosters critical thinking, problem-solving, and moral reasoning. For adults, the allegorical nature of the tales allows for deeper reflection on life's complexities and the consequences of one's choices.

The Panchatantra and Hitopadesha are widely available in various forms today.

Translations and adaptations can be found in libraries, bookstores, and online platforms.

Many free resources, including ancient manuscripts and modern interpretations, are accessible on digital archives and open-access websites.

For those interested in their original context, Sanskrit versions of the texts are also available, alongside translations in countless languages.

These stories, though written centuries ago, remain relevant because they touch on universal truths about human nature and society. They remind us that storytelling is a powerful tool for education, capable of blending morality, culture, and imagination into a single narrative. Including such insights in your book not only preserves this heritage but also ensures that future generations can learn from and be inspired by these timeless tales.

6-Step Actionable Strategy for Parents to Create Meaningful Bedtime Routines and Achieve Lifelong Results

1. Craft Personalized Stories for Your Child

Action: Every night, create a short, personalized story featuring a character that mirrors your child. Use a name that resonates with them and place the character in a setting they enjoy. Let the character face a challenge that is relevant to your child's life, such as learning to share, being brave, or facing a fear.

Result: This strategy will deeply engage your child's imagination and emotional intelligence. Over time, they will begin to reflect the virtues they see in these stories, such as courage, kindness, and patience.

2. Use Technology to Enhance the Storytelling Experience

Action: Leverage tools like AI assistants (ChatGPT, Google Gemini) to generate personalized stories. Provide specific prompts that include the desired story length, setting, moral, and challenges for the character.

Result: By using technology, you can effortlessly create unique stories that cater to your child's developmental needs. This reduces the stress of having to come up with a story every night and allows you to explore a vast array of ideas.

3. Involve Your Child in the Story Creation Process

Action: During the storytelling, pause and ask your child what they think will happen next. Encourage them to offer ideas, making them a part of the creative process. Adapt the plot based on their suggestions.

Result: This interactive element fosters creativity and decision-making skills. It will also help your child feel valued and connected, strengthening their emotional bond with you.

4. Integrate Simple, Fun Lessons into the Stories

Action: Each story should include a subtle lesson or value, such as the importance of good habits, honesty, or problem-solving. For example, a character might learn to brush their teeth regularly or show kindness to others.

Result: Children absorb moral lessons best through stories rather than direct instruction. These teachings will shape their behavior and character, influencing their interactions with others and their own self-awareness.

5. Create a Calming, Bonding Ritual

Action: Develop a consistent, relaxing pre-bedtime ritual with your child, such as a warm bath, a cup of herbal tea, or some quiet time together before the story begins.

Result: This predictable routine creates a sense of security and comfort for your child, promoting emotional stability. Over time, this nightly ritual will become something they look forward to, strengthening the parent-child connection.

6. Reflect and Reinforce the Story's Message

Action: After finishing the story, spend a few minutes talking about the moral of the story. Encourage your child to express what they learned and how it can apply to their own life.

Result: Reflecting on the story reinforces the lesson and helps your child internalize the values being taught. It also builds your child's self-confidence, as they feel equipped to face similar challenges in real life.

CHAPTER SIXTEEN

The Present Corridor: Finding Peace in the Chaos

In the hustle and bustle of daily life—managing busy schedules, meeting heavy workloads, tackling household chores, washing clothes, and cleaning up messes—we often live mechanically. Days pass by in a blur, leaving us without memorable moments or meaningful achievements. Without realizing it, we spend the most valuable resource we have: our time. And, as we go through life in this robotic way, our children observe and internalize it, believing that this is how life is meant to be. This inadvertently sends the wrong message to the next generation.

Stress, pressure, and responsibilities—yes, these are very real. The burden of life, high self-expectations, and things not going as planned can weigh us down. But what if we could set all of it aside, even for a little while, to truly enjoy the present moment?

Imagine a space in your life called the *Present Corridor*. This isn't just a physical space—it's a mental sanctuary, a dedicated retreat where time slows down, and your mind finds peace. Choose a specific corner of your home, workplace, or even a favorite spot outdoors, and declare it your Present Corridor. It could be as simple as a cozy chair by a window, a small corner with a soft rug, or even a section of your garden.

Once you've chosen this space, set an intention: whenever you are here, you will let go of work, distractions, past regrets, and future anxieties. Here, you will allow yourself to simply be—a moment of pause in the midst of life's chaos. This is where mindfulness begins, and it is far simpler than you may think.

To step into your Present Corridor, begin by sitting comfortably. Close your eyes and take a deep breath, drawing in the cool air as it moves through your nostrils and expands within you. Hold it for just a moment—not with force, but with gentle awareness. As you exhale, imagine releasing not only the air but also the weight of thoughts and emotions that no longer serve you. Repeat this cycle—inhale calm, exhale tension.

If your mind wanders, that's perfectly natural. Instead of resisting, acknowledge the thought and gently guide your attention back to your breath. Feel its rhythm. Notice how your chest rises and falls, how your body moves effortlessly with this unbroken cycle of life. Let yourself marvel at this simple yet miraculous process.

To deepen your experience, focus on your senses. Feel the texture of the surface beneath you, the temperature of the air on your skin, or the subtle sounds around you. Perhaps there's the faint rustle of leaves, the hum of a distant fan, or the rhythm of your own heartbeat. Ground yourself in these sensations, anchoring your mind to the present moment.

Make this practice easy and approachable by starting small—spend just two minutes here each day. Gradually, you can extend it to five, then ten minutes, as it becomes a natural part of your routine. You can also pair it with simple rituals to make it special: light a candle, play soft instrumental music, or hold a comforting object, like a favorite mug or a smooth stone.

Over time, you'll begin to notice a profound shift. This space, your Present Corridor, becomes more than just a physical spot—it becomes your personal oasis of calm. You'll start craving this time, not as an obligation but as a gift to yourself. Even a few moments here will begin to ripple through your life, making you more patient, present, and in tune with yourself and others.

And the beauty of this practice? It doesn't have to be perfect. Some days, your mind might wander more than others. That's okay. Mindfulness isn't about silencing your thoughts completely—it's about creating a space where you can meet them with compassion and let them pass like clouds in the sky.

In this sanctuary of your Present Corridor, you'll discover that the silence is not empty. It's full of life—of presence, of connection to something greater than yourself. This is where true mindfulness begins, not as an abstract concept but as a lived experience, one breath at a time. By creating this space for yourself, you're not just finding peace—you're learning to carry it with you into the rest of your life.

Your child, observing your calm and peaceful state, will naturally be drawn to your pure and serene energy. Children are incredibly intuitive—they can sense subtle changes in your mood and energy. When they see you relaxed and centered, it gives them a sense of safety and warmth. They will instinctively gravitate toward you, curious about the tranquility you're radiating. Without a word, they'll feel the transformation in you and, in turn, an effortless connection.

Invite your child to share this sacred space with you. Make it an experience they look forward to, even if they don't fully understand it at first. You could sit together, hold their tiny hands, or let them rest their head on your lap. Take slow, deep breaths together and guide them gently to focus on their breath or their senses. Ask them to listen to the sounds around them, feel the texture of the floor beneath them, or notice how the air feels on their skin. Keep it playful and simple—this isn't about forcing mindfulness but introducing it as a natural, enjoyable part of your time together.

You'll quickly realize that children are already attuned to the present moment. They live there, naturally and effortlessly, whether they're marveling at a butterfly or giggling at the sound of raindrops on the window. The real challenge lies in aligning your frequency with theirs—letting go of your distractions, worries, and to-do lists to step into their world. When you manage to do this, something magical happens. A divine connection forms between you and your child, one that words cannot capture. It's a bond rooted in shared presence, where love flows freely without the need for explanation or effort.

This connection will not only transform your relationship with your child but will also profoundly impact your sense of peace and purpose. You'll begin to see your child not just as someone you're responsible for but as a teacher who reminds you how to live in the now. Their laughter, curiosity, and wonder will become your guiding lights, pulling you deeper into the beauty of each moment.

However, taming your restless mind to enter the Present Corridor isn't always easy. Our minds are like mischievous monkeys, constantly leaping from one thought to another. At first, you might feel frustrated by how often your mind strays back to work emails or unfinished tasks. This is normal. Instead of resisting, "trick" your mind into cooperation.

Promise yourself, "Just 10 minutes, and I'll return to the chaos."

With time, your mind will begin to trust these moments of peace and willingly let go.

Be patient with yourself. Consistency is the key. Start with short sessions, even if it's just five minutes a day, and let the habit grow naturally.

Over time, this space will transform into a refuge—not just for you but for your child as well. It will become a sacred ground where you both can thrive, free from the pressures of the outside world.

In these moments together, you're not only fostering mindfulness but also creating lasting memories. Your child won't remember the screens or the toys; they'll remember the time spent with you, the comfort of your presence, and the peace you shared in your special corridor. And as this practice becomes a part of your daily life, you'll rediscover the profound beauty of simply being—together, in harmony, with nothing more than the present moment.

Six-Step Actionable Strategy for Creating a Blissful, Present Life

This six-step strategy is designed to help you shift your perspective and transform your environment into one of peace, mindfulness, and joy. By incorporating these practices into your daily routine, you'll experience a profound change in how you interact with the world and create a blissful space for yourself and your child.

Step 1: Designate Your Present Corridor

• Action: Choose a specific corner or space in your home or outdoors that will serve as your "Present Corridor." This space should be free from distractions like phones, work, or worries. It can be as simple as a cozy chair by a window or a peaceful spot in the garden.

• Why: Creating a dedicated space for mindfulness signals to your mind that this is a time to pause, breathe, and reconnect with the present moment.

Step 2: Set an Intention for Peace

• Action: Before entering your Present Corridor, set an intention to let go of stress, past regrets, and future anxieties. Tell yourself, "I am here to be present, to enjoy this moment, and to find peace."

• Why: Setting a clear intention helps focus your mind on what you wish to achieve, creating a mental sanctuary where peace becomes your priority.

Step 3: Begin with Simple Breathing

• Action: Sit comfortably, close your eyes, and take a deep breath in through your nose. As you inhale, feel the calmness filling you. Hold the breath for a moment and exhale slowly, imagining the release of tension. Continue this cycle for 2-5 minutes, focusing only on your breath.

• Why: Conscious breathing is one of the simplest forms of mindfulness, helping you to ground yourself in the present moment and calm the nervous system.

Step 4: Ground Yourself in the Sensory World

• Action: Engage your senses to enhance your mindfulness experience. Feel the texture of the surface beneath you, notice the temperature of the air on your skin, or listen to subtle sounds around you. Focus on one sense at a time.

• Why: Engaging your senses helps anchor your awareness in the here and now, preventing your mind from wandering into distractions.

Step 5: Invite Your Child to Join You

• Action: Invite your child to join you in your Present Corridor for a mindful moment. Hold their hand or simply sit together, breathing slowly. Encourage them to notice the sounds around them or feel the texture of the floor. Keep it playful and fun, letting them guide the experience.

• Why: Children are naturally attuned to the present moment. Sharing this experience deepens your connection with them and helps them learn the value of mindfulness.

Step 6: Cultivate Consistency and Patience

• Action: Start with just 5 minutes a day in your Present Corridor and gradually increase the time as it becomes a natural part of your routine. Be patient with yourself if your mind wanders. Allow it to drift, then gently bring it back to your breath and the present moment.

• Why: Consistency is key to creating lasting change. Over time, this practice will become second nature, and your mind will begin to crave these moments of peace.

The Shift in Perspective

By following these steps, you'll gradually change your perspective on life. No longer will you rush through your days, missing the beauty of the present moment. Instead, you'll embrace each moment as it comes, creating a peaceful, blissful environment that nurtures both you and your child. Over time, this practice will cultivate a sense of ecstasy, a deep connection to yourself, and a more meaningful relationship with those around you.

This approach not only improves your mental well-being but also creates a sense of harmony in your family, helping your child to thrive in an atmosphere of love, calm, and presence.

CHAPTER SEVENTEEN

Compassion

Parenting is a bit like running a relay race—but instead of handing your kid a baton, you're passing on your worldview, your values, and, let's be real, your quirks too. It's not just about raising a child; it's about shaping the future. And no pressure or anything, but the next generation will either save the planet or hoard crypto in underground bunkers, depending on the lessons we teach them today.

But let's zoom out for a second. When was the last time you thought about the big picture? Not just, "Did I pack the right snacks?" or "Why is there glitter on literally everything in the house?" but about what kind of world you're helping your child inherit. Look around—wars, greed, reality TV, and an endless hunger for more. It's like humanity collectively decided that compassion is optional and went all-in on chaos.

The tricky thing is, kids are little sponges. They're absorbing everything—how we talk to the barista, how we treat the cashier, how we handle a bad day. If they see us prioritizing our Amazon wish lists over helping a neighbor or choosing screen time over real connection, what do you think they'll learn? Spoiler alert: Not empathy.

Compassion in the Age of "More"

Let's be real—modern life isn't exactly a breeding ground for compassion. We're busy chasing promotions, upgrading our gadgets, and taking selfies with coffee cups like they're personality statements. And before you know it, we're raising kids who think kindness is as outdated as dial-up internet.

But here's the truth no one tells you: compassion isn't just about being nice; it's about being human. It's about recognizing that we're all in this messy, unpredictable ride together. And unless you've figured out how to survive on a private island with zero human interaction (or are Jeff Bezos), you need other people.

Yet, here we are, swiping through life like it's a dating app for happiness—more stuff, more success, more validation. And in this endless pursuit, we forget the stuff that actually matters: the hug you gave a friend on a bad day, the stray dog you fed because you couldn't just walk away, the plant you watered even though it looked like it gave up on life. These are the moments that quietly remind us what it means to be alive.

Kids Are Watching (And Judging)

Here's a fun fact: your kid is watching you more closely than a detective in a crime thriller. They're noting how you react when someone cuts you off in traffic, how you treat people who disagree with you, and whether you're genuinely interested in the world outside your bubble.

If they see you constantly chasing material things, obsessing over the latest gadgets, or scrolling endlessly on your phone while muttering, "Just one more minute," they'll think that's the norm. And before you know it, they'll be adults with the emotional depth of a potato, thinking kindness is an optional DLC in the game of life.

But here's the good news: kids are also incredibly forgiving. If you start showing compassion—even in small, clumsy ways—they'll notice. They'll mimic it. And eventually, they'll embody it.

Start Small, Think Big

Let's get something straight: changing the world doesn't mean you have to quit your job, join Greenpeace, or write inspirational Instagram captions about your "healing journey." It starts with tiny acts of kindness. Feed a hungry stray. Let someone merge in traffic without honking. Smile at a stranger (without looking like a serial killer).

These small actions create ripples. And when your kid sees you do them, they start to understand that life isn't just about personal gain—it's about connection. It's about realizing that the world isn't divided into "me" and "them." It's just "us."

The Paradox of Fulfillment

Here's the plot twist: the more you focus on helping others, the more fulfilled you feel. Weird, right? We spend so much time chasing happiness—more likes, more stuff, more everything—and it turns out the secret was giving, not taking. It's like discovering the last slice of pizza actually tastes better when you let someone else have it (still hurts a little, though).

And when your kid experiences this firsthand—when they see the joy that comes from giving without expecting anything in return—they start to internalize it. Suddenly, they're the ones sharing their toys, helping their friends, and looking for ways to make the world just a little brighter.

Leaving a Legacy

At the end of the day, parenting isn't about raising a kid who's good at math or sports or building the perfect Lego tower (though those are cool too). It's about raising someone who cares. Someone who looks at the world and thinks, "How can I make this better?"

When you embody compassion—when you live it, breathe it, and model it for your child—you're creating a ripple effect that can change the world. Because here's the thing: your child isn't just your responsibility. They're your legacy.

So, the next time you're tempted to brush off an opportunity to show kindness, remember: your kid is watching. And one day, when they grow up to be the kind of person who spreads light in a dark world, you'll know you played a part in that.

And honestly, isn't that better than any promotion, gadget, or perfectly curated social media post?

Compassion isn't just a choice—it's a superpower. Use it wisely.

Here are six effective steps that parents can take to effortlessly create a blissful environment and cultivate a compassionate mindset in their children:

1. Model Compassion in Everyday Interactions

Children are constantly observing their parents. Show compassion in your daily actions—whether it's offering help to a neighbor, being patient with a friend, or taking the time to listen. When your child sees you acting with kindness, they internalize that behavior as the norm. Simple gestures, such as helping someone in need, sharing, or being polite, are powerful lessons.

2. Practice Small Acts of Kindness Together

Make compassion a family activity. Encourage your child to help others in small ways, such as feeding stray animals, donating old clothes, or writing a thank-you note. Doing these acts together teaches your child that compassion is not just a concept but a way of living. Start small, but make it a regular practice.

3. Embrace "Compassionate Conversations"

Take time to discuss with your child the importance of empathy. Ask them how they think others might feel in certain situations. Guide them to consider the emotions of people around them, whether it's a sibling, a friend, or even a stranger. This helps them develop emotional intelligence and a deeper understanding of others' needs.

4. Encourage Generosity Without Expectation

Teach your child that giving is not about receiving something in return. Whether it's sharing toys, offering help to others, or donating, make sure your child understands that kindness and generosity bring joy because they are meant to help others, not to get something back. This will cultivate a spirit of selflessness and fulfillment in your child.

5. Create a Compassionate Environment at Home

Compassion starts in the home. Show patience, understanding, and empathy toward your child's needs and feelings. Allow your child to express themselves freely without judgment and help them navigate their emotions with understanding. A compassionate atmosphere at home reinforces the idea that compassion is not a rare, special act—it's a way of life.

6. Celebrate Acts of Compassion

Acknowledge and celebrate when your child demonstrates compassion, no matter how small the gesture. Praise their empathy and kindness with encouragement, which reinforces the idea that compassionate actions are valued. This positive reinforcement motivates them to continue acting with kindness and empathy in the future.

By implementing these six steps, parents can create a home filled with compassion that becomes second nature for their children. Over time, these simple yet profound practices can have a lasting impact on their worldview, fostering a generation that values kindness, empathy, and the joy of giving.

CHAPTER EIGHTEEN

Connection

The foundation of a blissful teenage life is laid during the critical years of a child's development, between ages 1 and 12. These formative years are when children learn trust, empathy, and self-worth, shaped largely by how they are treated by their parents. If a child is nurtured with patience, love, and understanding, they grow up feeling secure, valued, and emotionally connected. This creates a strong bond of trust between parent and child, which becomes crucial as they navigate the challenges of adolescence.

On the other hand, neglect, constant criticism, or lack of emotional connection in early childhood can lead to insecurities, resentment, and rebellion during the teenage years. Children who feel misunderstood or unsupported often turn to external influences, sometimes withdrawing from their parents entirely. The teenage years, often misunderstood as inherently difficult, are more a reflection of how a child has been treated earlier.

According to Some global research,

1. Teenagers Feel Alone, Even When Surrounded by Family

A study by SpringerLink found that 45% of teenagers hesitate to share personal struggles with their parents due to fear of judgment or misunderstanding. This means nearly half of the teens today are silently dealing with insecurities, dilemmas, or depression without seeking help at home.

Why?

• Parenting Mismatch:

Many millennial parents unknowingly focus on providing material comforts but fail to build emotional bridges. Teens often feel their emotions are dismissed with phrases like "You're overreacting" or "Everyone goes through this."

• The "Perfect" Parent Pressure: Many parents showcase perfection instead of vulnerability. Teens don't see their parents as someone who might understand failure, self-doubt, or trauma because they've never seen them talk about it.

2. Teen Depression and Anxiety Are Skyrocketing – And Parents Don't Know

According to the Pew Research Center, 70% of teenagers say anxiety and depression are major problems among their peers. However, only 30% of parents recognize these issues in their own children.

Teens often show subtle signs of distress, such as:

• Withdrawal from family activities

• Spending excessive time on their devices (which is often escapism)

• Sudden mood swings

What's worse? Many teens don't even have the vocabulary to articulate their feelings, let alone the courage to share them with their parents, who they perceive as "too busy" or "too controlling."

3. Teens Want Support, Not Solutions

A Stanford University study revealed that teenagers are more likely to open up to parents who listen actively and show empathy, rather than jumping to solutions.

Mistakes millennial parents often make:

• Trying to "fix" everything immediately: For example, if a teen says, "I hate how I look," many parents respond with, "You're beautiful!" instead of diving deeper into why they feel that way.

• Overreacting to small confessions: If a teen admits to failing a test or breaking a rule, they often receive disproportionate reactions. This discourages them from sharing in the future.

4. Trust Issues Start Early

Trust between parents and teens is built (or broken) during early childhood. If parents dismiss or invalidate their child's small concerns, it sets a precedent that sharing emotions is not safe.

For instance, a child who's told, "Stop crying over such a small thing," learns early on to suppress their emotions rather than express them. By the teenage years, this behavior solidifies into complete emotional withdrawal.

5. Teens Crave Genuine Connection Over Forced Rules

A Harvard Graduate School of Education report highlighted that teenagers who feel "seen" by their parents are:

• Two times more likely to involve them in life decisions.

• Three times more likely to share personal struggles, including dilemmas, traumas, and insecurities.

However, parents often focus on enforcing rules rather than creating meaningful conversations. For example, instead of a strict "No phones at dinner" policy, parents can encourage teens to share a highlight of their day.

A Wake-Up Call: The Cost of Ignorance

Every year, nearly 1.2 million teens globally commit suicide, according to the WHO. Many of these deaths stem from unresolved depression, anxiety, and a lack of connection with their families.

The reality is harsh: If parents don't step up now, their teens may grow up feeling unseen, unheard, and unsupported – leading to lifelong emotional scars.

The time to act is now. Teens aren't looking for perfect parents – they're looking for present ones.

"Parenting Beyond Authority: How Small Changes Can Save Your Relationship with Your Children"

Parents often believe that their bond with their children is unbreakable—a foundation so strong that no matter what happens, it will always hold. But reality proves otherwise. Adult children don't wake up one day and decide to cut off communication with their parents. This painful decision is usually the culmination of years of unresolved hurt, neglect, or mistreatment, despite their efforts to repair the relationship.

For many adult children, cutting ties with a parent isn't an act of rebellion—it's a painful choice made for their mental health. And while the consequences of this decision are heartbreaking, the most profound truth lies in this: It's preventable.

Parenting Is Not About Control, It's About Connection

Millennial parents grew up in a different world—one where obedience was prioritized over emotional understanding. They might unconsciously carry forward those same patterns: demanding respect, expecting compliance, and overlooking their children's feelings. But today's generation values connection over authority. If that connection is lost, even the strongest relationships can crumble.

Let's break this down with examples:

1. "You're Overreacting" – The Power of Emotional Validation

Imagine this: Your teenager comes to you in tears, saying their friend excluded them from a group outing. You dismiss it, saying, "You're overreacting. It's not a big deal."

What you think you're doing: Teaching them resilience.

What they feel: Their emotions don't matter.

Over time, repeated invalidation sends a clear message: "My feelings aren't safe here." By the time they're adults, they'll stop coming to you altogether—not out of defiance, but because they've learned you aren't emotionally available.

The Small Change: Validate their emotions, even if you don't fully understand them. Say, "That must feel really hurtful. Do you want to talk about it?" This shows that their feelings are valid and safe with you.

2. "I Sacrificed Everything for You" – The Danger of Conditional Love

Many parents, out of love and dedication, sacrifice their dreams, hobbies, and desires for their children. While this is noble, it can sometimes come with unintended guilt-tripping.

Example: Your child decides on a career path that you don't agree with, and you say, "After everything I gave up for you, this is how you repay me?"

What you think you're doing: Reminding them of your love and sacrifices.

What they feel: Your love is conditional on their compliance.

As adults, children who grow up in such environments often feel suffocated, resentful, or burdened by guilt. They may distance themselves to escape this pressure.

The Small Change: Express unconditional love. Instead of tying your sacrifices to their choices, say, "I'm proud of you for following your heart. My sacrifices were my choice because I love you, and I want to see you happy."

3. "I Know What's Best for You" – The Problem with Over-Control

Picture this: Your adult child wants to marry someone outside your community. You insist it's a mistake and push them to reconsider, saying, "I've lived longer; I know what's best for you."

What you think you're doing: Protecting them from a wrong decision.

What they feel: You don't trust their ability to lead their own life.

This dynamic creates a rift where the child feels they must either fight for independence or sacrifice their happiness to appease you. Over time, this constant power struggle can lead to estrangement.

The Small Change: Shift from control to guidance. Instead of dictating, say, "I trust your judgment, and I'm here if you need advice." This gives them space to grow while knowing you're always there for support.

4. The Silent Killer – Lack of Apologies

Parents are human, and mistakes are inevitable. But many millennial parents were raised in households where parents didn't apologize to children. This creates a cycle where mistakes are either ignored or justified, leaving the child feeling unseen.

Example: You lose your temper during an argument and yell at your child. Instead of apologizing, you say, "If you hadn't behaved that way, I wouldn't have yelled."

What you think you're doing: Explaining your behavior.

What they feel: Their feelings don't matter, and mistakes shouldn't be owned.

The Small Change: Model accountability. Saying, "I'm sorry for yelling—it wasn't right, and I'll try to do better," shows humility and teaches your child the value of taking responsibility for their actions.

Parenting: A Sacred Responsibility from God

Parenting is not just about raising a child; it's about shaping a soul. The trust your child places in you is a divine assignment, a bond given by God to guide, nurture, and uplift. Every word you say, every action you take, plants a seed in their heart—one of love, fear, resentment, or joy.

God entrusted you with this role not to control or dominate, but to reflect His unconditional love. How can we, as parents, mirror that love? By:
- Listening without judgment.
- Loving without conditions.
- Guiding without controlling.

When we parent with empathy, patience, and humility, we reflect the profound responsibility God has given us.

The Profound Impact of Small Changes

Every small action—a kind word, a listening ear, an apology—creates ripples in your child's life. Over time, these ripples form an unshakable foundation of trust and love. Conversely, neglecting these small moments leads to cracks that, if left unattended, can cause the relationship to crumble.

A Call to Millennial Parents

If you're reading this, take a moment to reflect:

• When was the last time you genuinely asked your child how they're feeling?

• Do they see you as someone they can talk to without fear of judgment?

• Have you apologize when you've been wrong?

Your relationship with your child isn't set in stone—it's a living, breathing connection that requires constant care. By making small, intentional changes today, you can prevent years of hurt and ensure that your child never feels the need to walk away for their mental health.

Parenting isn't about perfection—it's about presence. Be present, be kind, and be the safe haven your child deserves.

Based on your chapter "Connection," here are 8 actionable steps that parents can implement to foster a stronger, healthier relationship with their children. These steps emphasize long-term effort and are designed to create lasting changes, ensuring that parents not only strengthen their bond with their teens but also help them navigate emotional struggles effectively.

8-Step Strategy for Building Connection with Your Teen:

1. Create a Daily Uninterrupted Connection Time

Dedicate at least 15-20 minutes each day to be fully present with your teen. Ask open-ended questions such as, "How was your day?" or "Is there something on your mind you want to talk about?" Make sure to eliminate distractions like phones, and listen without judgment. This consistent time fosters emotional availability and strengthens your bond over the long term.

2. Be Vulnerable and Share Your Own Struggles

Teens need to see that their parents are real people, too. Share your personal stories of failure, insecurity, or tough times and how you overcame them. This vulnerability builds trust and reassures your teen that it's okay to not be perfect, which helps them open up more freely in return.

3. Validate Their Feelings Instead of Dismissing Them

When your teen expresses frustration, sadness, or insecurity, resist the urge to minimize their emotions with statements like, "You're overreacting." Instead, acknowledge how they feel, saying, "I understand why you're upset," or "That must be really tough." By validating their feelings, you create an emotional safety net where your teen feels heard and understood, which strengthens the emotional connection over time.

4. Shift from Control to Curiosity

Instead of enforcing rules without context, engage your teen in conversation about their experiences. If they're spending time on their phone, ask, "What's something exciting you discovered online?" This approach fosters curiosity and prevents the defensive walls that often form between teens and parents. It encourages your teen to share more, which deepens your relationship.

5. Normalize Mental Health Discussions

Make mental health a regular part of family discussions. Share stories of people overcoming challenges, talk about your own mental health struggles (if applicable), and frame therapy as a healthy tool for self-growth. Normalize the conversation to remove the stigma, allowing your teen to feel comfortable discussing their feelings without fear of judgment or punishment.

6. Celebrate Effort, Not Perfection

Teenagers often feel they can't live up to the perfection expected of them. Instead of applauding perfect grades or flawless performances, focus on their effort and resilience. For example, say, "I'm proud of how hard you worked," or "Mistakes are part of learning. What did you learn from this?" Celebrating progress over perfection builds their confidence and removes the pressure to be perfect.

7. Apologize When You Make Mistakes

Show your teen that accountability is vital by apologizing when you've made a mistake or acted out of line. Saying, "I'm sorry for yelling earlier; I should have been more patient" teaches them the value of humility and self-reflection. This encourages them to take responsibility for their actions and nurtures an environment of mutual respect.

8. Be Consistent and Patient

Building trust and emotional connection is a long-term process. Change doesn't happen overnight. Be patient with yourself and your teen as you implement these practices. Expect small improvements over time rather than instant results. Recognize that fostering a strong bond requires ongoing effort, but every small step will cumulatively have a powerful impact on your relationship.

Conclusion:

The strategies outlined above may seem small, but their cumulative effect is profound. Your efforts to make these changes consistently will gradually build a strong foundation of trust, empathy, and mutual respect that lasts far beyond the teenage years. By staying patient and persistent, you will see your relationship with your teen grow, making it easier for them to share their struggles and lean on you for support.

CHAPTER NINETEEN

Heritage: The Invisible Backpack You Pass On

Think about life as a video game. Every decision you've made, every mistake you've learned from, every level you've painfully cleared, has added tools to your inventory. Now, here's the plot twist: without even realizing it, you were handed some items when you started the game—beliefs, habits, and quirks that came pre-installed, courtesy of your parents and surroundings. That's your heritage, the invisible backpack of traits and values passed down to you, whether you asked for it or not.

Let's get real for a moment. Ever find yourself saying something and immediately thinking, "Whoa, that sounded exactly like my mom/dad"? Maybe it's the way you scold someone for not turning off the lights ("Electricity doesn't grow on trees!") or your tendency to overthink every decision. Guess what? Your parents are living rent-free in your brain. Their belief systems, unconscious habits, and worldviews seeped into you like an accidental software update you didn't sign up for.

But here's the kicker: now that you're aware of it, you hold the cheat code.

Imagine you're not just a player in this game but a game developer too. As a parent, you have the rare chance to build the next player's experience. You can consciously pack your child's invisible backpack with tools that actually work, rather than ones that glitch out halfway through life's challenges.

Let's talk about the power of conscious parenting. You get to sort through your personal encyclopedia of life lessons—the ones you learned through heartbreaks, sleepless nights, and embarrassing mistakes—and decide what to keep and what to ditch. It's like Marie Kondo-ing your belief system: does this mindset spark joy (or resilience or empathy)? If yes, pass it on. If not, leave it behind.

The "Heritage Lab"

Picture this: life is a research lab. Your parents were the OG scientists, conducting experiments with love, discipline, and some questionable tactics (remember when they said eating carrots would make you see in the dark?). They tried things, failed, adjusted, and—whether they meant to or not—passed down the results of those experiments to you.

Now, as the next-gen scientist, you get to take their findings, refine them, and create a new manual for your child. And here's the cool part: your child doesn't have to waste years figuring out what you already learned. They get the highlight reel—the good stuff—without slogging through the bloopers.

For example, maybe you learned the value of patience the hard way—waiting tables at a crowded café where every customer seemed determined to ruin your day. Now, instead of sending your child to a café for "character-building," you can weave patience into their daily life through stories, games, and conversations. You become the human shortcut, saving them from unnecessary detours.

Think of heritage like your family's Spotify playlist. Some tracks are absolute bangers—values like honesty, hard work, and kindness. Others? They're the cringe-worthy songs you'd rather skip (like that generational tendency to bottle up emotions or avoid tough conversations). Your job is to curate the playlist your child will listen to on repeat, carefully mixing timeless classics with fresh beats.

Or take Instagram filters. You inherited a default filter for viewing the world—one shaped by your upbringing. But now, you can choose to swap it for one that's clearer, brighter, and less judgmental. As you "edit" your perspective, you're also editing the filter your child will inherit.

Every life lesson you've earned, every moment of self-reflection, is like laying a brick in the foundation of your child's future. This is your chance to build a legacy—a solid, enduring structure they can stand on. Think of your child as an architect. They'll design their own life, but your lessons are the blueprints that guide them.

And here's the beauty of it: when you parent consciously, you're not just shaping your child's heritage—you're reshaping your own. By breaking generational cycles, embracing new perspectives, and nurturing your child's potential, you're creating a ripple effect that stretches far beyond your family.

So, ask yourself: what hard-earned lesson can you turn into a priceless gift for your child? Whether it's resilience, empathy, or the art of saying "no" without guilt, you have the power to save them years of trial-and-error.

Remember: Heritage isn't about perfection. It's about giving your child the tools to face life with confidence, clarity, and compassion—and maybe a little humor too. After all, the world can be a chaotic place, but with the right invisible backpack, they'll be ready for anything.

Here are five key actions parents can take to make the process of passing on values, lessons, and heritage smooth and enriching for their child:

1. Lead by Example (Be the Blueprint)

Children learn more from what they see than what they're told. If you want to instill honesty, empathy, or resilience, you need to model those qualities in your own life.

Action: If you want your child to manage emotions constructively, start by showing how you handle stress—calmly discussing problems, practicing mindfulness, or seeking solutions without blaming others.

2. Communicate Mindfully

Conversations are the foundation of a child's belief system. Talk openly about your experiences—your struggles, successes, and lessons learned. This will help your child connect your values to real-life situations.

Action: During family dinners, share one moment from your day where you acted according to a core value (e.g., courage, patience) and explain why it mattered.

3. Encourage Curiosity (Not Blind Compliance)

Instead of expecting blind acceptance of your beliefs, encourage your child to ask questions and form their own understanding. This fosters critical thinking and helps them internalize lessons more deeply.

Action: If your child asks, "Why do we save money?" instead of saying, "Because I said so," explain the importance of financial security, use examples, and invite them to create a savings goal of their own.

4. Create Learning Opportunities Through Stories and Experiences

Stories and hands-on experiences leave a lasting impact. Use them to reinforce important values in a relatable, engaging way.

Action: Share personal or fictional stories where the main character learns a value (like persistence). You can also involve your child in real-life activities, such as volunteering, to teach kindness and empathy.

5. Reflect, Refine, and Stay Flexible

Your child is unique, and not every value or lesson will resonate the same way. Regularly reflect on what's working and refine your approach as needed.

Action: Observe how your child responds to your teachings. If they're resisting or not understanding, try another approach—like turning lessons into games, discussions, or collaborative activities.

By embodying these actions, parents can ensure that the values they pass on become not just lessons but lifelong tools for their children.

Final Thoughts

Dear Reader,

As you turn the final page, take a deep breath and feel the weight of what you've just accomplished. This book has been a journey—one that started with a simple idea and grew into something so much bigger. You've not only read these words, you've embraced them, pondered them, and most importantly, you've reflected on your own parenting journey. You've become part of a movement that is transforming how we see the art of raising our children.

Parenting isn't just about guiding the next generation; it's about realizing that you, as a parent, are the creator of their future. The lessons you share, the values you instill, and the love you pour into their lives are the very building blocks of a new world. You are shaping not just their lives, but the world they will inherit. And that is an immense power—one that deserves to be celebrated.

I want to take a moment to express my deepest gratitude to you for choosing this book, for trusting me with your time, and for believing in the message within. It's no small feat to reflect on one's parenting and make the shifts necessary for growth. Your commitment to becoming a conscious, empowered parent is inspiring. And in doing so, you are not only changing the future for your child but for generations to come.

The road ahead may not always be easy. But as you move forward, know that you are equipped with the most powerful tools: love, patience, perspective, and a deeper understanding of the immense impact you have on shaping the world. The future is in your hands, and the power to create a better one starts right here, with you.

Now, I urge you to share this book. Share it with your family, your friends, and fellow parents. Let's make this perspective on parenting a ripple that reaches far and wide. This book might not have invented new parenting truths, but the perspective it offers is something worth considering—a lens through which we can view parenting with more compassion, intention, and vision.

Thank you from the bottom of my heart for allowing me to accompany you on this journey. Your belief in this book, and in yourself as a parent, is the true magic that brings these words to life.

May your parenting journey be filled with joy, growth, and countless moments of bliss. You are the creators of the future, and I have no doubt that your children will flourish under your loving guidance.
With all my love and gratitude,
Dipak Khushalani

About The Author

Dipak Khushalani

Dipak Khushalani is an educator, storyteller, and father dedicated to helping parents raise curious, compassionate, and visionary children. With years of experience as a Physics teacher, he understands how a child's learning journey is shaped not just by formal education but by the environment parents create at home.

His personal journey—from guiding his own daughters to storytelling as a parenting tool—led him to write Roots and Wings. This book is not just about reducing screen time; it is a holistic guide to childhood development, covering modern homeschooling methods, nurturing curiosity, storytelling, patience, the role of food, and mindful parenting techniques.

When he's not writing or teaching, Dipak enjoys exploring new ideas in education, sharing childhood stories with his daughters, and finding ways to make learning fun for young minds.

Connect with Dipak:

? Email: dnkhushalani@gmail.com